THE ATL PRESS PRESENTS

TRUMP *this.*

The day all immigrants left America.

ANONYMOUS WRITER

THE ATL PRESS

Atlanta, GA.

© THE ATL PRESS

THE ATL PRESS, Atlanta, GA.

Published 9-11-2019

www.TheATLPress.com

ISBN: 978-1-7923-1470-4

Library of Congress Cataloging-in-Publication Data

#2019946302

TRUMP *this.*

1. Politics 2. Government 3. Congress

 4. President 5. Donald Trump

Printed in the United States of America

Table of Contents

America, the land of opportunity, the powerhouse of all countries, the one place where dreams could become true has fallen from grace.

Now the land of disgrace, a home to illegal immigrants from "Sh*t hole countries". Where men could become women and women transform into men. Our allies and enemies alike laugh in our face. They want no parts of this God forsaken place.

This country that publicly punish and chastise God fearing people who declare it's wrong for same sex marriage. Some in their ignorance even claim that it's a hate crime and try to compare it to racism.

Law enforcement kill at will and minorities are usually the victims. Where white supremacy rules the narrative, no matter the platform.

Black lives matter but doesn't all other's matter too?

Can we "Make America Great Again"? A slogan used by Reagan, Clinton and now Trump. Illegal immigrants cost American taxpayers billions each year but building a wall will only cost a fraction of that. Is it wrong for them to want a part of the American dream as well? The hard truth is, if America builds the wall, crime will fall. But that's the least of our problems.

1

TRUMP

Long before Hillary Clinton, Bernie Sanders, Marco Rubio, Martin O'Malley, Jeb Bush, Ben Carson, Chris Christie, Ted Cruz, Lindsey Graham, Mike Huckabee, John Kasich & George Pataki thought about running for the 2017 Presidential election, they, like most of America held a mental relationship with Donald Trump.

Trump's entire life before becoming president was to build and brand an empire. No matter the rhetoric about his business acumen, the TRUMP brand has been etched in our memory's way before November 2016. Bush and Clinton with their lineage didn't even stand a chance and as far as marketing goes, they were the only two that had the brand power to challenge him.

The other candidates were popular in their states but these three carried a name known the world over.

To many voter's, Donald Trump represented change from the normal White House politics. A change that was needed and the experience to run America like the business that it once was or supposed to be. We figured that his White House staff could assist him with the political matters that he wasn't savvy on and that Trump could implement certain business strategies that would benefit America's businesses and strengthen our economy. This would intern trickle down to the working-class citizens and entrepreneurs.

Unfortunately, several inhumane events took place that changed the narrative in America. Hate crimes and public displays of racism headed too many media headlines fueled by police brutality and acts of terrorism. President

Trump's responses to these inhumane acts caused an uproar and the opposing party begun to associate the "Make America Great Again" slogan with racism. But aren't we all a little racist in our own way, would we be better off in our countries of origin? It's obvious that we all can't get along.

How would America look if all the immigrants went back home? Would there be less crime? Would there be more jobs? Would that make America great again? Tell me, what do you think? Here's what I think!

2

What if all the blacks left?

Let's start by being very honest with ourselves. How do you really feel when you look at a black person? Do you feel empathy? Do you feel sorrow? Are you embarrassed by them and their actions? Do you see a proud culture of people? Would you trade places with any black person today? If so, which ones? If not, why? Do you see blacks as first or second-class citizens?

When I speak of blacks, I'm referring to any black American citizen of African descent. African Americans, Nigerians, Ethiopians, Eritrean, etc.

African Americans make up around 14% of the U.S. population. Most African Americans arrived here by way of the slave trade and took root in the southern states like Alabama, South Carolina, Georgia, Mississippi, North Carolina and Virginia during 1776 – 1865. Slavery only ended legally, 154 years ago. The descendants of these slaves along with legal African immigrants has gone on to contribute to both the improvement and demise of America.

William Edward Burghardt Du Bois was the first African American to earn his doctorate from the University of Berlin and Harvard, he became a sociology professor at Atlanta University and was one of the founders of the NAACP in 1909. Other black scholars such as Angela Davis, Cornel West, Henry Louis Gates, Jr., Toni Morrison & Lerone Bennett, Jr. contributes and contributed to America's educational system within their own vocation.

Black's it seems has been blessed with unbelievable athletic abilities. They run faster and jump higher than any other race in America and maybe the world. Any non-black American is most definitely in awe or envious of this spectacular gift which can make them inferior to the black athlete. Basketball players; Bill Russell, Kareem Abdul-Jabbar, Wilt Chamberlin, Magic Johnson, Michael Jordan, Kobe Bryant and LeBron James are among a few black athletes whom elevated their sport. Football players; Jim Brown, Walter Payton, Doug Williams, Deacon Jones, Lawrence Taylor, Michael Irvin, Deion Sanders, Warren Moon, Terrell Owens, Randy Moss and Jerry Rice left their imprint on the NFL along with hundreds of other black football players.

Jackie Robinson, Satchel Paige, Ken Griffey Jr., Barry Bonds, Willie Mays, Hank Aaron, Reggie Jackson and Frank Thomas were among hundreds of black baseball players that decided to leave it all on the field when it came to the game of major league baseball. "America's past time".

The black community introduced several delicious dishes to the American food industry known as Soul Food. With mouthwatering entrees like collard greens, sweet potato pie, banana pudding, smothered pork chops, fried chicken, black eye peas, fried fish and lima beans. Any American can make the above dishes but it's all in the soulful seasoning and cooking of the recipes that makes it soul food.

You can find several soul food restaurants throughout certain neighborhoods across the U.S.A. Although it may taste good, it's also said to be a main cause of high blood pressure and diabetes among the African American's. The excessive consumption of pork, salt, butter and sugar can also lead to heart attacks if not monitored and eaten in moderation. According to Cardio Smart; African American adults are up to two times more likely to develop high blood pressure by age 55 compared to whites.

When it comes to business, a few names stand out among African Americans. Madam C.J. Walker whose birth name was Sarah Breedlove introduced a line of beauty products for black women in 1910 and became one of the first female millionaires. John H. Johnson made his bones as a publisher and found success by launching the Johnson Publishing Company founded in 1942. His most noted titles include the Ebony and Jet magazines, both are staples in the African American community.

John Merrick made millions as an entrepreneur and hit pay dirt by launching the North Carolina Mutual Life Insurance Company in 1898. Merrick went on to open several businesses in the Raleigh, Durham North Carolina area known then as "The Black Wall Street" while expanding North Carolina Mutual Life Insurance Company throughout the South.

Robert Sengstacke Abbott founded "The Chicago Defender "newspaper in 1905 as a newspaper publisher and practiced law as an Attorney. Berry Gordy, founder of Motown records created a sound that touched all races with artist like "The Supremes", "The Temptations", "Jackson 5", "Smokey Robinson" and "Diana Ross".

This trend inspired modern day African American entrepreneurs like Don Cornelius, Quincy Jones, Oprah Winfrey, Russell Simmons, Sean Combs, Percy Miller, Curtis Jackson, Sean Carter, Daymond John, Tyra Banks, Nick Cannon, Shaquille O'Neal, Kanye West, Will Smith, Byron Allen and many more.

Have you ever thought about who invented the items that you use every day? Like the refrigerator that you use to store your food and beverages. The can that holds your canned goods, the jelly you spread on your toast or the soap you wash with every morning? Well, have you?

Lewis Howard Latimer along with John Nichols invented a lightbulb with a carbon filament. The original light bulb had a paper filament created by Thomas Edison that burned out quickly. Latimer's carbon filament lasted extremely longer. You'll probably using it to read this book right now.

Our law enforcement, rescue departments, environmental inspectors and military all need certain equipment in order to survive daily. One of the most important items is the gas mask. Garrett Augustus Morgan, Sr. invented the gas mask as a unit that would protect the user from toxic gases and pollutants. Working around or being exposed to hazard materials, chlorine gas, biological agents or mustard gas would be impossible without the gas mask.

Frederick McKinley Jones designed a very important component for the trucking industry. His portable air-cooling unit for trucks enabled the industry to store and carry perishable food. Jones went on to receive several patents for more inventions to include the starter generator and rotary compressor.

Marie Van Britten Brown and her husband Albert L. Brown created the first closed-circuit television security monitoring system. George Franklin Grant; dentist and the first African American professor at Harvard invented a wooden golf tee. Many African American's invented countless other invention's that contributed to the fabric of America, yet we still operate on an affirmative action system.

It was said that African American men commit nearly half of all murders in the U.S.A. According to research posted on channel 4.com, black people are involved in more crimes than other races and therefore they commit more crime. Thus, explaining why blacks get shot and killed more by police than other races.

In the last few years the number of black men and women shot by police officers in the U.S.A. has become a common occurrence. The current racial divide seems just as bad as it was in the early 60's. It makes you wonder if we were better off during segregation. At least the blacks had their own economic system within their communities and the whites had theirs. Maybe the answer to the racial divide is to divide. This way everyone would know where they stood, and the blacks could keep all that crime in their own neighborhoods, and we could eliminate this affirmative action.

Middle class citizens along with the 1% in America has often voiced their concern about their tax money being spent on public housing for blacks and minorities. But according to huduser.gov the percentage of minorities in public housing isn't what you think. 40% of public housing units are occupied by people 65 years or older whom live alone. But if this 40% of 65-year-old public housing occupants need the assistance of a government housing program along with their social security checks to live. Then we have a problem, no matter the race.

Households with children make up 43% of public housing. 12% of the homes are occupied by nonelderly disabled. Blacks make up 48% of these households while they only occupy 19% of renter households.

According to the census bureau (2012), blacks made up 41.6% of welfare program users. African Americans make up less than 20% of the U.S. population and still take the lion's share of welfare compared to other races. The problem seems to be unemployed, under paid and noneducated blacks, the culmination of these factors will always lead to government assistance. Maybe it's time America finds a way to educate these people, so that they can be more productive and not dependent. But as you read earlier, there's hundreds of black scholars, business owners, entrepreneurs and inventors, so whose fault is it that they're unemployed and uneducated.

When you look at the data, it's easy to believe the stereotypes. "Blacks are lazy", "They refuse to work", "The women have tons of kids so that they can get more government assistance". Rumor has it that women on welfare are denied help if a man is found in the household? So, if the women get boyfriends or even starts to date, the guys can't stay over. If they do and the governing body of the welfare program finds out. Said program will end the assistance. I found this to be ridiculous, it has to be a rumor.

The Supplemental Nutrition Assistance Program also known as SNAP is another way to say Food Stamps. Blacks fall next to last on the low-income poverty chart just above Native Americans. SNAP pays millions to low income African Americans a year, so that they could have adequate food to eat. Damn, isn't America great! The government will give you money for food if you don't have enough cash and provide housing if you can't afford a place to stay. So, what is all the complaining about?

African Americans spend $1.2 trillion annually in the American marketplace according to Nielsen. Rumor has it that blacks waste their money on material goods. Is it because they can't afford the valuable or meaningful items? Among the top yearly purchases are shelf-stable juices and drinks with $1.04 billion spent, detergents at $829.8 million, bottled water at $810.3 million, frozen unprepared meat &

seafood at $761.7 million and personal soap and bath needs at $573.6 million, all necessities.

Most of the government assistance programs were created many years ago but things are different now. The entire corporate structure has changed for the better, there more career opportunities and the entrepreneur class continues to innovate in amazing ways. Maybe it's time to scale back on the government assistance, it seems to enable bad habits and laziness. America can use that money to build the wall.

The United States has the largest prison population in the world. More than 2.4 million people are inmates, over half that number consist of inmates with drug crime sentences for 1 year or more. According to the ACLU, America with only 5% of the world's population has 25% of the worlds prison population. We are the world's largest jailer. 1 in every 99 adults are living behind bars, 1 in every 31 adults are under some form of correctional control, counting prison, jail, parole and the probation population.

Of the incarcerated, black men are 6 times more likely than white men to be in prison. An extremely large amount of these inmates are housed in private prisons. These facilities are places where individuals are physically confined or interned by a publicly traded company that is under contract by a corporation or government agency. These companies enter into contractual agreements with said entity who in turn sends them prisoners to house. The entity in turn pay the prison's an agreed amount each day or per month for housing that inmate.

If you would like to invest in these companies, you can do so by contacting your stockbroker or using an online system like Etrade to purchase stock. The most popular of these publicly traded companies are *"CoreCivic formerly Correctional Corrections of America whose trade symbol is CXW"*, *"The GEO Group, inc. whose trade symbol is GEO" and "Community Education Centers whose trade symbols are CEC was purchased in 2017 by The GEO Group"*. Isn't America a great place to live when you can make a profit off incarcerated convicts? Make sure that you purchase a few shares today!

It seems that blacks are a commodity within our American way of life. It's obvious that someone stands to make a profit whenever a black person is incarcerated, maybe that's why the police are always locking them up. But who makes money if you kill them? If they conjured up the fortitude to go back to Africa would that make America a better place to live?

When they leave; the private prison's will be losing trillions in contracts, there will be a smaller police force, the murder rate would decrease tremendously along with gang violence and drug crimes. The sports industry will suffer a big lost in track and field, football and basketball which will decrease profits from ticket sales, endorsements, television contracts, etc. The music industry as we now know it will become debunked while the American market in whole would lose a few trillion in consumer dollars. Would that make us great again?

America is a reactive nation; we don't find a way to fix problems until we know that a problem exists. I.e. in the early years, cigarette smoking was allowed in restaurants, on airplanes during flights and in all public places until smokers and non-smokers begin dying from cancer that also affected non-smokers, 9/11 – caused airport security (TSA) to tighten up on their travel guidelines. The fear lies in the present, while you think everything that Trump is saying or doing is wrong. It will be too late, later when you realized that he was right all along.

3

9/11

America the home of the free and land of opportunity has its flaws. We are a divided nation, be it economical, racial or gender based. It is very normal to go about your everyday business and not greet a stranger in passing or even on a crowded elevator. There you are in a box full of people for at least 2 minutes and no one is greeting each other, you reach your floor then you exit. No have a nice day or have a nice morning, you leave with this negative energy and carry it with you throughout the day.

We are constantly being fed negative news and images 24 hours a day, controlling our thoughts and how we react with certain people. We have red zoned neighborhoods for the poor, gated communities for the rich and the middle class fall somewhere in between. Luxury cars, suits and jewelry are used to give us status among our peers no matter how we obtained it. The rich look down their noses at the have nots and the have nots always seem to pay a poor people tax. Homes, cars, gas, food and health care cost more in poor neighborhoods while the opposite is true in more affluent neighborhoods. No matter who you vote for, things seem to remain the same, congress can't and won't unanimously agree on anything.

On 9/11 when the towers were attacked and hundreds of Americans died, we became one, if only for a moment. Every breathing American felt pain and empathy for those that were murdered. When you saw a stranger on the street you spoke and felt their energy, no matter their race or sex. We mourned together as human beings, it seemed everyone was in unison then.

4

Gay Pride.

The current climate in America is alive and well when it comes to gays. There was once a time in America when you could turn on the TV and watch a music video during primetime hours and see guns until it started influencing teenagers to purchase and use guns, the words "Shit" or "Bitch" could only be heard on movie networks, now there scripted to be heard on primetime TV.

Cartoons in the early 70's, 80's and 90's like Tom & Jerry, Popeye, Ren & Stimpy, etc. portrayed violent acts until kids started imitating those acts in real life. The entertainment industry with its thirst for the gay dollar doesn't have any guidelines in place to protect children viewers who have no clue about what it is to be gay. This unfairly influences our children subconsciously and is not fair to them or their parents. I think the industry should create a rating symbol to notify viewers of any gay content. After all, most of the population isn't gay and doesn't want to be. If everyone were gay, who in the hell would be left to procreate?

Celebrating someone because they're gay or homosexual is equivalent to adultery, incest, rape & murder. It's a cardinal sin. America, we have the narrative all wrong. These falling beings should be asking their most high for forgiveness not acceptance. The United States has become Sodom and Gomorrah blinded by the sodomites, what follows is our destruction. Within the minds eye of the inhabitants of the most holy soil we are a target.

Pride shall come before the fall. Like a herd of sheep without their shepherd they shall continue to bump their heads until they acknowledge their sins, repent and ask the almighty for forgiveness. They shall not enter the Kingdom of God until they cast away this abomination and those that knowingly promote and force this sin on God's people shall receive the same fate. For it is not prideful to be gay and never will be in the eyes of our Lord.

5

What if all the Caucasians left?

Caucasians or white people are of European descent. According to the 2016 census, white Americans make up 61.3% of the United States population, they are the majority of all the races but not superior by any means, yet conspiracy theorist would like for you to believe that.

Ask yourself this question. How could a superior race be told what to say and what not to say when it comes to a word. What other race do you know of has this problem? The N word or the word nigger has caused hundreds, if not thousands of white people to lose their jobs and careers just because evidence was provided, proving that they used the word at one time or another. Do you know of any black people whom got fired for using the word nigger? They can use it all they want to, and nothing will happen to them. Now, do you call that white supremacy?

But let us not forget what white Americans contributed or contributes to this country. During the 17th century while European powers were colonizing North America, they brought with them their ideas on education. American forefathers; Thomas Jefferson and Benjamin Franklin were among the few that challenged this idea of European education before they eventually settled on what parts of the system to use and what parts to disregard. Educational reformer Horace Mann dedicated his life to promoting public education. His most noted words of the 1800's was; "it is the law of our nature to desire happiness. This law is not local, but universal; not temporary but eternal. It is not a law to be proved by expectations, for it knows no exceptions".

When it comes to white athletes there's a talented list, let's start with the great Babe Ruth a baseball legend. Jerry West, Bill Walton, Larry Bird & John Stockton left big impressions on the game of basketball. Bart Starr, Roger Staubach, Joe Montana, Don Marion, John Elway, Terry Bradshaw, Joe Namath & Peyton Manning took the game of football to unimaginable heights during their careers.

Rumor has it that white people love bland food. Items such as potato salad, poached halibut, kale and any other non-seasoned food, can be associated with clean eating. This type of eating lowers the chances of high blood pressure, high cholesterol and obesity. Could this contribute to the reason that Caucasians are not high on the hypertension list? I guess the right question would be; what is white people food? Is there such a thing? I mean the blacks have soul food, the Indians have their food, Hispanics have their food, the Italians have their food, the Japanese and Chinese have theirs. So, what is Caucasian food?

Many titans of industry came from white America. John P. Morgan the Connecticut financier and banker dominated the corporate financial industry during the 1800's. He's also credited with the merger that led to General Electric GE whom was formally Edison General Electric and Thomson-Houston Electric Company. John D. Rockefeller; Oillionaire, business magnet, philanthropist and industrialist was said to be the richest man in America while alive and the oil industry (BP, Exxon, Amoco, Mobil) carried on his legacy once he died at the age of 97 in 1937. Warren Buffett; American investor, philanthropist and businessman is the third wealthiest person in the world with a net worth of $84.9 billion.

He currently sits as chairman and CEO of Berkshire Hathaway a multinational conglomerate holding company. The company owns industry giants such as Duracell, GEICO, Dairy Queen, Fruit of the Loom and Helzberg Diamonds to name a few. BH also hold large stakes in United Airlines, Delta Airlines, Pilot Flying J, Kraft Heinz Company and American Express. This is what makes America great, that anyone could achieve this same success if they really wanted to.

Warren Buffett is the example that all modern entrepreneurs and businessmen, women look to. Aren't we all just one decision away from taking that first step towards our dreams and goals? The hard truth is, no! In America there is such a thing as white privilege. White men are more privileged than anyone, no matter the race or gender. You only need to tune in to your local news, grocery store, work, etc. to see it. For all of you non-white readers; I challenge you to get professionally made up to look like a white man and venture out into your city for a few hours, you will be amazed at the experience.

Where would we be without Thomas Edison? He invented the phonograph, motion picture camera and the light bulb. The world would be dark, without music and movies, hypothetically speaking. Great white inventors like Edison changed not only America but the world. When you take a closer look, the white's that created most of the inventions were not from America, like Einstein & Tesla. Two of our most prominent are Bill Gates and Steve Jobs but are they inventors or contributors?

Thomas Edison was known for hiring aspiring inventors to work on an idea as a group. This practice would become a normal way of business for many moving forward. Let's face it, Henry Ford didn't invent the automobile, but he improved it by using the assembly line method which was invented by Ransom E. Olds to mass produce cars.

Alexander Fleming invented antibiotics (Penicillin) although he was white, he's not American, he was born in the UK. Sir John Harington invented the toilet but he like Mr. Fleming was not American, he was born in England. Johannes Gutenberg a German inventor invented the printing press not a white

American. The internet was invented by a group of very diverse and talented people not by just one white American.

Dutchman Zacharias Jannsen invented the microscope. John Vincent Atanasoff was a blue-blooded New Yorker, a white American credited for inventing something that changed the way of life as we knew it when he invented the first digital computer back in the 1930's. This would lead to the modern-day pc. Many white people have contributed great inventions, but it seems most of them were not American's.

According to the 2016 FBI: Uniform Crime Report, white American's committed 67.6% of rape crimes, 68.4% of burglaries, 69% of larceny & theft, 66% of motor vehicle theft, 72% of arson, 59% of violent crimes, 68.7% of property crime, 65.5% of forgery and counterfeiting, 67% of fraud, 68.4% of vandalism, 61.4% of embezzlement, 71.6% of sex offenses, 71% of drug abuse violations, 67.1% of offenses against family and children, 66% of vagrancy crimes and 82.2% of driving under the influence. Since white American's represent the largest of our population it would only make sense that they commit more crimes. Whites come second to blacks when it comes to inmates here in American prisons. Anti-prison activist would have you think that whites make up the lowest race incarcerated in American prisons.

Currently white Americans make up 20% of public housing occupants, only 4% behind black Americans. The media feeds into the race narrative, often placing whites in the upper class of citizens when the reality is more economic than racial. When you hear; section 8, the projects or even public housing. The first image that comes to mind isn't white Americans. Everything that we see, read or hear about low income housing sticks to that narrative. It's as if the media wants you to think that white people are above public assistance or welfare. America doesn't discriminate when it comes to aiding its citizens, it's one of the many reasons that this is an awesome place to live.

In a study done by Lexington law it shows that white Americans receive more food stamps than any other race at 36.2% and 43% of the Medicaid recipients were also white. The previously mentioned statistics clearly show that not all white Americans are rich or even middle class. A lot of white's fair the same or higher among other races when it comes to poverty, low paying jobs and committing criminal offenses. Yet white families have 10 times the net worth of black families. Does this make white American's lazy?

As of 2018 according to research by catalyst, white American's control $12.1 trillion worth of buying power in the U.S. and lead all races with 82.1% of America's buying power. If all white American's decided to leave the United States today, America would become a third world country.

The economy would miss the $12.1 trillion in spending money, food not so much. Corporate giants like Ford, Chase, Berkshire Hathaway, Apple, Wal-Mart, Starbucks, etc. would cease to exist. Our law enforcement as we know it would become depleted because white Americans make up most police officers. Several crimes would decrease by large percentages, i.e. D.U. I's, rapes, burglary, fraud, forgery & counterfeiting, sex offenses, embezzlement, arson, motor vehicle theft & vagrancy crimes to name a few.

6

Cut from a different cloth

One of the biggest misconceptions in United States politics is that you need a law degree and or a military background to run for political office. To run for president, you must be at least 35 years old, born in the U.S. and maintain citizenship for 14 years. You must also be a registered voter. 1 office term is 4 years and there is a 2-term limit. There are no other qualifications, to win you only need to be elected by the people. Isn't America great!

Trump obtained a Bachelor of Science in Economics at The Wharton School. He made his bones as an international real estate developer, businessman and television personality. The only military experience Donald J Trump has, came from his enrollment at the New York Military Academy for his 8th to 12th grade years.

Former presidents, Obama, Bush, Clinton and Reagan all held prior political office's in their home states while Trump built hotels, casinos and skyscrapers globally. While his political competitors voted on laws and mingled with lobbyist in D.C. before they decided to hit the presidential campaign trail. Trump was calling in favors from political animals whom benefited from previous donations and business alliances that he helped formed. The Donald publicly stated during his presidential campaign that "as a businessman and real estate developer, when I called on certain politicians they answered every time".

Maybe this explains why Trump is hated by both the democrats and some in the republican party. He truly represents the people, not government. His days of dealing with politicians gave him insight on how shady politics really are. Trump knows who took money and or favors from him in the past. He understands that America is a business and it needs to return to prominence and the status quo won't get it done. Those shady politicians just never thought that he would be on their side of the fence. The game has changed, and Donald Trump knows where the bodies are buried.

7

The Immigration and Naturalization Act, 1965

"This bill that we will sign today is not a revolutionary bill. It does not affect the lives of millions. It will not reshape the structure of our daily lives, or really add importantly to either our wealth or our power. Yet it is still one of the most important acts of this Congress and of this administration. ... This bill says simply that from this day forth those wishing to immigrate to America shall be admitted on the basis of their skills and their close relationship to those already here."

-President Lyndon B. Johnson

Preference categories

Family preferences

The Immigration and Naturalization Act of 1965 and subsequent legislation established preference categories for individuals seeking visas to reunite with their families in the United States. These categories are listed below in descending order, with the highest preference category listed first:

1. Immediate relatives (including spouses, unmarried minor children, and parents) of U.S. citizens
2. Unmarried adult children of U.S. citizens
3. Spouses and minor children of lawful permanent residents
4. Unmarried adult children of lawful permanent residents
5. Married adult children of U.S. citizens
6. Brothers and sisters of U.S. citizens

Professional preferences

The Immigration and Naturalization Act of 1965 and subsequent legislation established professional preference categories for individuals seeking visas. These categories are listed below in descending order, with the highest preference category listed first:

1. "Persons of extraordinary ability" in the arts, sciences, education, business, or athletics
2. Individuals holding advanced degrees or possessing "exceptional abilities in the arts, science, or business"
3. Skilled workers with a minimum of two years of training or experience; unskilled laborers for permanent positions
4. Other special classes of immigrants, including religious workers, employees of U.S. foreign services posts, and former U.S. government employees
5. Individuals investing between $500,000 and $1 million "in a job-creating enterprise that employs at least 10 full-time U.S. workers"

8

What if all the Chinese left?

Chinese are the third largest foreign-born immigrants in America. They fare well when it comes to holding positions in education. One stands out, Amy Lynn Chua currently holds a position as the Law Professor at Yale Law School which followed her 7-year tenner at Duke Law School, Chua earned her BA & JD from Harvard College & Law Schools. Jim Chen currently holds a position as the Professor of Constitutional Law at Michigan State University College of Law. The Chinese population only makes up a very small percentage of the professors and educators in America.

Michael Chang was the youngest male tennis player to win a Grand Slam tournament. Karen Chen, figure skater is the 2017 U.S. National champion, 2015 CS Golden Spin of Zagreb bronze medalist & the 2016, 2017 CS U.S. Classic bronze medalist. Ivana Hong, artistic gymnast was a member of the 2007 World Artistic Gymnastics Gold medal American team & bronze medalist at the 2007 Pan American Games. Chinese Americans sports skill set seems to lean more towards gymnastics, ice skating, tennis & poker.

Chinese food has woven itself into American culture, a buffet or fast food restaurant can be found in every neighborhood on every other corner no matter the neighborhoods income level. The next time you visit a Chinese restaurant, take some time to observe the foot traffic and while observing make a mental note of the number of Chinese patrons you see patronizing the restaurant. The outcome may shock you.

American taste differs from native Chinese, because of this the Chinese adjusted the flavors of their authentic dishes to fit American taste and culture to appeal to the masses. Among these trailblazers are Andrew Cherng, founder and chairman of Panda Restaurant Group (Panda Express). His net worth is currently $3.1 billion and growing, Andrew and his Father franchised the Chinese food experience for everyone to enjoy. Roger H. Chen founded 99 Ranch Market the largest Taiwanese American supermarket chain in the U.S.

Popular dishes include, Sesame chicken, Pepper steak, General Tso's chicken, Crab Rangoon, Fried wontons, Almond chicken and much more. Most American's think about fried chicken wings, sweet & sour pork, fried rice, egg rolls and fortune cookies when you mention Chinese food or take-out but most of that isn't authentic.

Business moguls, Ken Lin founder of Credit Karma, Look Tin Eli co-founder of the Canton Bank of San Francisco, Himalaya Capital Management founder and investment banker Li Lu, Albert Chao co-founder of Westlake Chemical, Perry Chen co-founder of Kickstarter and Steve Chen co-founder of Youtube are among many Chinese American's considered to be titans of industry, most of their ideas and hard work have changed the course of America.

Credit Karma and Youtube for example has become tools used in everyday life. The idea of American immigrants is based on this exact principal, to create businesses and 10 or more jobs for American citizens. If you live in the

United States as a legal immigrant, you're expected to be a great citizen and or business professional, that's the trade-off.

Inventor An Wang and founder of Wang Laboratories made life easier for everyone with the development of desktop calculators and the first word processors. Flossie Wong–Staal most noted for her achievements in AIDS research has dedicated her life to discovering a vaccine to prevent the AIDS virus.

Chinese (Asian) Americans fall in the lowest percentile when it comes to crimes compared to other races. They make up 7.3% of gambling crimes, 5.7% of prostitution and commercialized vice crimes and 2% of sex offenses. Keep in mind that this percentage includes all Asian Americans.

In the scheme of things these crimes are very closely related to organized crime. The Chinese mafia better known as the TRIAD has become infamous in U.S. cities such as San Francisco and New York. These organizations specialize in prostitution, fraud, money laundering, extortion, trafficking, smuggling and counterfeiting goods. The criminal gangs are major players in the global illegal drug trade and are responsible for smuggling chemicals from Chinese factories to the U.S. to produce methamphetamine.

When it comes to counterfeiting, they hold no punches; currency, expensive books, watches, DVD's & designer apparel are some of their biggest money earners. The numbers of 2.1% may seem small in comparison to the other 97.9% of Americans here in the U.S... Chinese Americans representing that 2.1% fare average among other minority races when it comes to poverty and collecting food stamps, welfare, etc. 3.9% of Asian Americans are on household assistance.

14.4% of the American Chinese population are living in poverty. According to Pew Research Center in 2016, Asians displaced blacks as the most economically divided racial or ethnic group in the U.S. This may come as a surprise because every time we see a homeless person on the corner, at the gas station, sleeping under a bridge or on a park bench. We see mostly white and or black people.

America without Chinese people will survive but we'd miss their food, the restaurant's and take out, great inventors and business professionals. There will be no Credit Karma or Youtube. We'll experience a huge reduction in illegal drugs, mostly meth while counterfeiting, prostitution & sex trafficking crimes plummet to all-time lows along with the elimination of the Chinese organized crime families.

9

I didn't vote for TRUMP!

The one place where American's can practice being true American's is in the voting booth. We walk in then select our preferred candidates. It is then our decision to share our choices with whom we choose to or not, it's our choice.

The current political climate of America has many Trump voters clamming up, afraid to admit that they voted for him. Not because they're ashamed of voting for him but they fear for their lives due largely in part to how some of the media portrays the president.

Our discretion in the voting booth will prevail once again in the upcoming election. American's at heart want a pure red-blooded candidate with morals who's not afraid of the media or congress. We need a president that wants to build a wall to protect our borders, we need a president that understands the need to protect our businesses, we need a president that understands the art of negotiating with allies and enemies, we need a president that has no fear, we need a president that wants to Make America Great Again!

10

What if all the Greeks left?

It's estimated that Greek Americans make up close to 3 million of the U.S. population. Strangely it seems like all the Greeks live in New York, Chicago or Boston but their contribution to America reaches across the nation. At least three of America's prestigious Universities' has had Greek presidents. John Brademas was president of NYU from 1981-1991, Peter Diamandopoulus served as the president of Adelphi University from 1985-1997 & Constantine Papadakis served as the president of Drexel University from 1995-2009.

In the world of sports, the Greeks dominate in more ways than one. When you think of Greece, you envision Olympic stadiums, chariots, and Greek Gods. What if I told you that the names have changed but the Greeks still hold a tight rein within the sports arena. Peter Angelos a successful product-liability lawyer and former basketball player currently owns the Baltimore Orioles of MLB. Ted Phillips is currently the CEO and president of the Chicago Bears of the NFL. Dean Spanos owns the Los Angeles Chargers of the NFL. Peter Karmanos, jr. currently owns the Carolina Hurricanes of the NHL.

Theodore John Leonsis is the majority owner, chairman and CEO of Monumental Sports & Entertainment, which owns the NHL's Washington Capitals, NBA's Washington Wizards, NBA G League's Capital City Go-Go, WNBA's Washington Mystics, and the AFL's Washington Valor and Baltimore Brigade. Monumental Sports also owns the Capital One Arena in Washington, D.C. and manages the Kettler Capitals Iceplex and George Mason University's EagleBank Arena.

The list of great Greek American athlete's is longer than you may think. It includes; Pete Sampras who made his career as an all-time great pro tennis player. Nick Markakis, outfielder for the Baltimore Orioles of MLB. Niko Koutouvides, linebacker for the Denver Broncos of the NFL. Chris Chelios, player for the Detroit Red Wings of the NHL and Dave Batista, professional wrestler of the WWE.

The American Greek community is well known for their cuisine. Greek restaurants and eateries can be found in every major city through-out the U.S. Their most popular foods include; lamb, salads, olives, cheese, yogurt, pita bread, gyros, lentil soup and sword fish. Most Greek dishes are healthy for you unlike the cuisine from other races. It doesn't cause high blood pressure, high cholesterol or diabetes like soul food does.

Greeks fare at the top of the list when it comes to business. Nickolas Davatzes created both the A&E Network and The History channel. James N. Gianopulos sits as the chairmen and CEO of Paramount Pictures. Theodore Sarandos, jr. is currently the chief content officer for Netflix. George Skouras was president of United Artist while his brothers; Spyros was president of 20th Century Fox & Charles was president of Fox Coast West. Christos Cotsakos is the co-founder of E-Trade, Jamie Dimon sits as chairman and CEO of JPMorgan Chase. John Paul DeJoria is the co-founder of John Paul Mitchell hair products. Ed Zander sits as the CEO of

Motorola, Dean Metropoulos is the owner of Pabst Blue Ribbon company. William Tavoulareas is the president of Mobil Oil Corporation.

We Americans have Leo Stafanos to thank for inventing the delicious Dovebar. George Ballas changed the lawn industry when he invented the weed eater.

But when it comes to crime and especially organized crime, we seem to always overlook the Greeks. Like many of the other races, they have their share of crime. Amongst the crimes committed are illegal gambling, extortion, racketeering and loansharking.

One of the most infamous American Greeks, Chelsais "Steve" Bouras terrorized the city of Philadelphia as the boss of the Phila Greek Mob during the 70's. His crime family flooded the streets with methamphetamines and extorted 100's of families and businesses throughout Phila. They even controlled the Phila gun trade along with drug trafficking and murder.

The poverty level for American Greek families with children under the age of 18, rates at 8% of the U.S. population and 4% of the unemployment rate. Would you believe that at one time in America the Greeks were discriminated against just like the black's? In store windows, signs were posted that read "No Greeks Wanted". The infamous KKK included them on their list beside the niggers and the Jews. They wanted all Greek women to be sterilized and didn't want them to mix with White Americans.

Murdered, beaten and bruised; Greek American's proved to be a resilient race by becoming successful business owners, professionals and good citizens. The Greeks fare in the lowest percentile when it comes to purchasing power in the U.S. If they were forced to leave America, we would miss their cuisine and businesses while experiencing a decrease in drug trafficking & murder crimes.

11

Undocumented.

What most American's don't understand or get, is their place in the United States and what it means to its infrastructure. On your birthday you were issued a birth certificate and registered into the hospital's database of newborns. Soon after your parents took you home, they made plans to get you a social security number so that you would be recognized as an American citizen.

After a few months passed by, they took you to get your immunization shots, so that you wouldn't get infected by any fatal viruses or diseases. Life goes on then you learn how to crawl, walk, talk and before you knew it you were attending kindergarten with other new little people like yourself. When your parents enrolled you in kindergarten, they provided the administration with your proof of citizenship documents; social security card, shot records and birth certificate then your name was entered into the board of education's database. From this point on every move you made within the educational system was documented. If you and your parents moved to a different city and you attended a new school, that was documented, if you got into a fight with a fellow student and was told to report to the principal's office. Yes, that was also documented as a disciplinary report, warning, suspension, etc.

These documents followed you from kindergarten, elementary school, middle school, high school and college. If you deviated from the educational path and got arrested and found yourself in jail. Yes, those school reports also followed you to the courts because they showed a track record of your past behavior. If you skipped college and went directly to work and found a job, you were introduced to the IRS, FICA and any other American agency that was there to collect on your debt. What debt?

That would be the cost you were going to pay the rest of your life as a U.S. citizen. You find yourself in adulthood away from your parents and living in your own home; paying rent, bills and buying groceries. During your life you will repeat these steps until your last breath, the ideal of America will not survive without it. If you pay your bills on time, you can apply for credit which will place you in a situation to afford more but with interest. This is the value you add to America as a documented citizen.

Imagine not being documented, being home schooled, not having a birth certificate or social security number. You will be able to move freely about the United States without paying taxes, you can use any name you want because no one really knows who you are and you can commit crimes with reckless abandon, you really don't even exist according to the infrastructure of America.

It will be easy to find good work in construction, landscaping, hospitality and more jobs in similar sectors where you can get paid cash under the table. There you will find more people like yourself who will expose you to more underground jobs and network's that were put in place for you to survive off the grid while being undocumented.

12

What if all the Indians left?

The Indians were here before the idea of America, in fact this is their land. We are all immigrants except for them! There 310 Indian reservations across the United States. In efforts to apologize or make up for taking the Indians land the U.S. put several organizations in place to monitor this big issue. One of the first was the "Office of Indian Trade"; its main objective was to maintain the factory trading network of the fur trade. After a 16-year run the Office of Indian Trade ended and caused tension between the native American's and immigrants.

Two years later the Bureau of Indian Affairs was formed and remains in operation today. It was created to monitor and organize relations between the native Americans and United States government. The Indians and their reservations remain separate from the American government and all its laws. This would be the new way of life moving forward but the new Americans (that's us) wanted all the land and its treasures, all to ourselves.

To accomplish this task, we murdered, robbed, raped and destroyed everything that the native American's or Indians held dear. The native Americans are a resilient people, so it's no surprise that they eventually started to receive reparations. We took all the land that we could and made this country our own, these are the principals that the United States were built on.

As a proud American this is a hard pill to swallow but how can you not like what America has become. We are the land of opportunity and if that took destroying the lives of thousands of native Americans in the process then I guess someone had to pay the price. That disgusting feeling that you have in your gut right now because of what you just read. My friend, that's how it feels to be a god damn American!

Down but not out the Indians have contributed more than you know to this United States of America. Craig Womack, *Creek -Cherokee*; took on a mission to educate people about his heritage and currently holds a position as professor of native American Literature at Emory University. Paul Chaat Smith, *Comanche*; sits as an associate curator at the National Museum of the American Indian. Most noted

Charles Eastmen, *Santee Dakota*; attended Boston University and assisted in forming the Boy Scouts of America while forming 32 native chapters of the (YMCA) Young Men's Christian Association. The native Americans, oddly are viewed as immigrants in the eyes of America when it comes to racism, education, ownership, crime, etc. This also makes the opposite side of the spectrum true. Indians have benefited from what America has to offer; I think they're better off because of the opportunities.

Hall of Fame baseball player, Johnny Bench, *Choctaw*; blessed millions of MLB fans during his career as a pro baseball player with the Cincinnati Reds. Edward "Wahoo" McDaniel, *Choctaw-Chickasaw*; entertained millions of wrestling fans as a professional wrestler with the National Wrestling Alliance. Angel Goodrich, *Cherokee*; entertained millions of basketball fans as a WNBA player with the Seattle Storm and Tulsa Shock. Notah Begay III; *Navajo*; made a name for himself as a professional golfer on the PGA Tour and spent time as an analyst with NBC Sports and the Golf Channel.

Native American cuisine goes unnoticed in America but most of us consume it every day. Corn can be eaten several ways through a native American process called nixtamalization which transforms the corn into meal and or harmony. Grits, cornbread, whiskey and liquor are all made with corn. Several other vegetables were adopted from the Indians; potatoes, pumpkin, squash, tomatoes & sassafras are just a few.

Indian meats consisted of rabbit, possum, squirrels, dear, duck, salmon, seafood, seal, moose, bird eggs and raccoons. Some other wild resources included acorns which was grounded into flour, mushrooms, sunflower seeds and pine nuts. For fruit the natives ate wild berries such as huckleberries, blackberries, raspberries and muscadine grapes. Animal skin, fur and intestines were used to make clothing while the bones were used to make weapons, making use of every part of the slaughtered animals.

Sharice Davids, *Ho-Chunk*; U.S. attorney and democratic politician was elected to congress in 2019 for Kansas 3rd congressional district. Republican; Ben Reifel, *Brule Lakota*; sat as U.S, representative for South Dakota's 1st congressional district. Debra Anne Haaland,

Laguna Pueblo; attorney and politician was elected as democratic U.S. representative for New Mexico's 1st congressional district. Most noted native American Sequoyah, *Cherokee;* invented the Cherokee syllabary which was used to write the Cherokee language in 1810 and early 1820's.

Compared to white and black women, 34% of native American women suffer sexual assault in the United States mostly committed by white men according to the National Violence Against Women Survey. Alcohol abuse rates are at an all-time high on Indian reservation when compared to the United States population according to research on native American alcoholism.

The conviction rate for criminals are very low on the Indian reservations unlike the rate on American soil. Could this be a result of what happens when you govern yourself. America unlike the sovereign reservations fully has a criminal system designed to punish criminals. The BIA aka the Bureau of Indian Affairs acts as the law enforcement agency for these reservations but are they really?

One can only imagine what America would be like if it were only inhabited by the native Americans. Once you take away all that we immigrants have contributed, only the essentials would remain and maybe that's enough. Millions of trees would still tower across the plains, pollution and global warming absolutely would not exist. Eliminate skyscrapers, housing developments, automobiles, guns, the financial system, fancy clothes, shoes and jewelry. Processed foods, healthcare, the education system, electronics, lights, plastic, rubber, the military, law enforcement, casinos, hospitals and universities would be non-existent.

When you put it in perspective the native Americans should be very thankful that things turned out the way they did. Sure, they suffered in the beginning, but progress comes at a cost no matter if you wanted it or not. In exchange for their pain they received reparations, so we don't owe them anything. Many of them are wealthy beyond what they could ever imagine. They don't even have to pay sales or property taxes if they live on a federal Indian reservation. Isn't America a great place to live!

13

Bankrupt!

A Chapter 11 business bankruptcy is designed for businesses that has a chance to turn things around. It's not such a bad thing when your business is headed towards failure. One must wonder why a lot of failing businesses haven't taken advantage of this valuable tool. In this plan the company reorganizes and continues business under a court-appointed trustee. This trustee may also be the owner of the business.

The business then files a detailed plan on how it can reorganize and pay off its debts to its creditors. From there, the creditors will vote on the plan. The courts will approve the plan if they find it fair and equitable. Reorganization plans provide for payment to creditors over some period, which can exceed 20 years or more.

President Trump filed bankruptcies during some of the worst times in America's economy. During the gulf war his businesses suffered the same as many other businesses during this period, but he probably lost a lot more money.

If some of the other business owners who experienced a downturn during the gulf war had filed for Chapter 11. Maybe they would still be in business at this time.

The media would have you label Trump as a bad businessman but he's quite the opposite. He just knows how to play the game and use the rules to his advantage. Let's not confuse Chapter 11 bankruptcy with personal bankruptcy, Trump has never filed Chapter 7 or personal bankruptcy. In the sum of things this is an awesome move. A move by one of America's greatest players. If you plan on playing the game, you must know all the rules and when and how to use them to your advantage.

14

What if the Indian Americans left?

The Indians originating from India have planted firm seeds here in America. Har Gobind Khorana is one of the most noted Indians that resided in America. The biochemist had the pleasure of sharing the 1968 Nobel Prize for Physiology or Medicine with Robert W. Holley and Marshall W. Nirenberg. Venkatraman Ramakrishnan shared the 2009 Nobel Prize in Chemistry with Ada Yonath and Thomas A. Steitz.

Alexi Grewal won the Olympic Gold medal in cycling and remains the only American to do so. Gymnasts Mohini Bharadwaj Barry won two NCAA titles while attending UCLA. Gymnast Raj Bhavsar proved to be one of the best in America when he became a member of 2001 U.S. World Championship Team. Brandon Chillar became a professional NFL player for the storied Green Bay Packers and St. Louis Rams.

One of the most notable Indian contributions here in America, is their cuisine. Decorated with rich spices and herbs, it is however an acquired taste. Indian restaurants can be found in most major cities where there's an Indian culture. Some Americans find it hard to stomach the hot spices and herbs. Many of these dishes have gone mainstream and made its way into our kitchens from lentils, atta to pearl millet.

Traditionally, India like Africa eat with their right hand (no silverware) as eating with the left is considered disrespectful. This is probably because they wipe their asses with their left hand. Can you imagine sitting at the table eating dinner and someone digs in with their left hand and grabs a hand full! How disgusting! In America we love our toilet paper, no one wants a pile of shit on their hands or in their fingernails.

It's also Indian tradition that a family sticks to its calling or family business. If your family is known for growing produce than the rest of your family will grow produce as well. Maybe this is the reason that so many Indians named Patel own a big percentage of the hotels here in America. I doubt very seriously that they are all kin, but it does give off the perception of unity which in turn equals power.

As of 2015, Indians owned 22,000 of the hotels and motels in America. I wouldn't compare these hotels/motels to the Hilton's, Westin's or Marriott's here. Some may rank among the top tear but most fall way below the 2-star mark due to subpar upkeep, bad location and bad customer service. Unlike most American business owners who run their day to day business during the day then go home to retire for the rest of the day, most of the Indian hotel/motel owners take up residency at their hotel or place of business.

This may be a frugal business move from their perspective, but it gives off a very bad vibe to its potential customers. Leaving subpar rooms to be booked by prostitutes, drug fiends and other unsavory characters. Some locations do better than others depending on its zip code, but the result is still money and I guess that's all that matters.

A large percentage of convenient stores and gas stations are also owned by Indians. From Chevrons, Exxon's, 7 Eleven's, Indian Americans own over 80,000 of these stores here in the United States. We frequent the stores daily and probably know at least one owner by name or facial recognition. Gas stations are essential to our way of life and these immigrants are leading the nation in ownership. To date they are the richest ethnic group in America surpassing white Americans.

Amar Bose the founder of the famous (1964) Bose corporation launched one of the first Indian American owned companies and has trailblazed the way for his culture. Many of us has founder of Innovations Ventures LLC; Manoj Bhargava to thank for giving us that *5-hour Energy* boost that's found on every gas station counter. Women can thank the co-founder of *Chippendales*; Somen Banerjee for providing them with some alternative entertainment.

Indian Americans hold several CEO positions at major U.S. companies to include; Indra Nooyi, CEO of PepsiCo, Satya Nadella, CEO of MicroSoft, Rajeev Suri, CEO of Nokia, Sundar Pichai, CEO of Google, Shantanu Narayen, CEO of Adobe Systems, Ajay Banga, CEO of MasterCard and Ajit Jain, CEO of Berkshire Hathaway Reinsurance Group. The Indians are definitely among the most productive citizens in America contributing to the business, education and medical sectors.

Like other immigrants the Indians also fall victim to racism and hate crimes here in America. Unfortunately, terrorist events on American soil and abroad has brought unwanted attention to some Indian Americans whom had nothing to do with the crime except for their resemblance to the culprits. Their Islamic practices spread globally, so it was no incident that hate crimes against Indians increased soon after the 9/11 attack.

American's were in shock for years after this horrific event. The land that we know, and love had been attacked by someone that resembled a race living here on our very soil. Someone had to know something! The Indians had access to chemicals, digital information, company trade secrets, owned most of the gas stations and had family members living in the very countries that launched the attacks against us. What would you have done? If there is one race that has its reasons to threaten our way of life, it's the Muslim Indian Americans.

If the Indians returned to their home country India, America will lose largely in a few sectors, or will we? Over half the gas stations you see today will not be there or will not be owned by Indians. The hotel/motel industry will suffer the same fate. Many companies will lose their sitting CEO's and will be left to replace brilliant minds along with a hard work ethic.

The cuisine will probably not be missed. The medical field will suffer greatly because they will have thousands of great doctors to replace. College enrollment would drop tremendously in the medical, science, technical and financial fields, etc.

15

No Human Trafficking on Our Roads Act.

On January 8, 2018; president Trump signed Act S.1532. The report reads as follows.

```
115th Congress
Report
                              SENATE
 1st Session
115-188
```

NO HUMAN TRAFFICKING ON OUR ROADS ACT

R E P O R T

of the

COMMITTEE ON COMMERCE, SCIENCE, AND TRANSPORTATION

on

S. 1532

November 30, 2017.--Ordered to be printed

_____

U.S. GOVERNMENT PUBLISHING OFFICE

79-010   WASHINGTON :
2017

SENATE COMMITTEE ON COMMERCE, SCIENCE, AND TRANSPORTATION

one hundred fifteenth congress

first session

JOHN THUNE, South Dakota, Chairman

ROGER F. WICKER, Mississippi   BILL NELSON, Florida
ROY BLUNT, Missouri   MARIA CANTWELL, Washington
TED CRUZ, Texas   AMY KLOBUCHAR, Minnesota
DEB FISCHER, Nebraska   RICHARD BLUMENTHAL, Connecticut

74

TRUMP this...

JERRY MORAN, Kansas   BRIAN
SCHATZ, Hawaii
DAN SULLIVAN, Alaska   EDWARD
J. MARKEY, Massachusetts
DEAN HELLER, Nevada   CORY A.
BOOKER, New Jersey
JAMES M. INHOFE, Oklahoma   TOM
UDALL, New Mexico
MIKE LEE, Utah   GARY C.
PETERS, Michigan
RON JOHNSON, Wisconsin   TAMMY
BALDWIN, Wisconsin
SHELLEY MOORE CAPITO, West   TAMMY
DUCKWORTH, Illinois
    Virginia
CORY GARDNER, Colorado
MARGARETWOODHASSAN,NewHampshire
TODD C. YOUNG, Indiana
CATHERINE CORTEZ MASTO, Nevada
                Nick Rossi, Staff
Director
            Adrian Arnakis, Deputy Staff
Director
            Jason Van Beek, General
Counsel
            Kim Lipsky, Democratic Staff
Director
        Christopher Day, Democratic Deputy
Staff Director

TRUMP this...

115th Congress	}	
{	Report	
		SENATE
1st Session	}	
{	115-188	

===

NO HUMAN TRAFFICKING ON OUR ROADS ACT

_____

November 30, 2017.--Ordered to be printed

_____

Mr. Thune, from the Committee on Commerce, Science, and Transportation,
submitted the following

R E P O R T

[To accompany S. 1532]

[Including cost estimate of the Congressional Budget Office]

The Committee on Commerce, Science, and Transportation, to
which was referred the bill (S. 1532) to disqualify from

operating a commercial motor vehicle for life
an individual who
uses a commercial motor vehicle in committing
a felony
involving human trafficking, having considered
the same,
reports favorably thereon without amendment
and recommends that
the bill do pass.

Purpose of the Bill

The purpose of S. 1532, the No Human
Trafficking on Our
Roads Act, would provide a lifetime ban from
operating a
commercial motor vehicle (CMV) for an
individual who uses a CMV
in committing a felony involving a severe form
of trafficking
in persons.

Background and Needs

Current law prohibits an individual from
operating a CMV if
the individual is convicted of any of nine
different enumerated
offenses, including alcohol abuse, negligent
manslaughter, and
drug trafficking. The proposed legislation
would add a felony
involving a severe form of trafficking in
persons to the list
of disqualifying offenses, and like a
controlled substance
violation (49 U.S.C. 31310 (d)), the
disqualification would be
for life.
    Human trafficking, particularly sex
trafficking, is known
to be present at commercially operated truck
stops and State-
operated rest areas throughout the United
States. Given their

remoteness and insulation from communities, these locations can
be a convenient place for sex traffickers to operate with
minimal concerns for detection. The frequent movement of
victims aids traffickers both in maintaining control of the
victims and avoiding law enforcement. For example, victims who
work in fake massage businesses are often rotated between
cities so they do not establish relationships and seek help.
Other forms of human trafficking, such as labor trafficking,
have a presence in the trucking industry as well.
    Nonprofit organizations like Truckers Against Trafficking
(TAT) have made substantial progress in spreading awareness of
areas where human trafficking and the trucking industry
intersect. Their efforts have resulted in increased reporting
of trafficking incidents by truckers, the eyes and ears of
roads nationwide. For example, the Committee heard testimony at
a July 12, 2017, human trafficking hearing on how the trucking
industry is an important part of the solution, including saving
lives by identifying instances of human trafficking.
    Despite these important efforts, more can be done to combat
human trafficking, and this bill would serve as an important
deterrent measure, in addition to penalizing traffickers.

Summary of Provisions

S. 1532 would disqualify, for life, an
individual who uses
a CMV in committing a felony involving a
severe form of
trafficking in persons from operating a CMV.

Legislative History

S. 1532 was introduced by Senator Thune
(for himself and
Senators Klobuchar and Nelson) on July 12,
2017. Senators
Cornyn, Rubio, Heller, and Blumenthal are also
cosponsors. On
August 3, 2017, the Committee, by voice vote,
reported S. 1532
favorably without amendment.

In addition, on July 12, 2017, the
Committee held a hearing
entitled, ``Force Multipliers: How
Transportation and Supply
Chain Stakeholders Are Combating Human
Trafficking,'' which
examined the various interactions between the
transportation
sector and human trafficking, and served as an
opportunity to
explore some of the specific solutions and
efforts utilized by
organizations that work to mitigate the
exploitation of
individuals.

Estimated Costs

In accordance with paragraph 11(a) of rule
XXVI of the
Standing Rules of the Senate and section 403
of the
Congressional Budget Act of 1974, the
Committee provides the
following cost estimate, prepared by the
Congressional Budget
Office:

S. 1532--No Human Trafficking on Our Roads Act

S. 1532 would permanently prohibit anyone who has used a commercial vehicle to commit a felony involving human trafficking from operating a commercial motor vehicle in the future. Based on information from the Federal Motor Carrier Safety Administration (FMCSA), CBO estimates that implementing the bill would have no significant effect on the federal budget.

State agencies that issue driver's licenses would be responsible for implementing the prohibition in the bill. Based on information from FMCSA, CBO expects that the agency would need to change policies and procedures as well as update the training that it offers for state inspectors and investigators who are responsible for combating criminal activities such as drug and human trafficking. For such work, CBO estimates that the agency would require about half the time of one full-time employee annually over the 2018-2022 period. CBO estimates that implementing the provisions of the bill would cost less than $500,000 over the 2018-2022 period; such spending would be subject to the availability of appropriated funds.

Enacting S. 1532 would not affect direct spending or revenues; therefore, pay-as-you-go procedures do not apply. CBO estimates that enacting S. 1532 would not increase net direct

spending or on-budget deficits in any of the
four consecutive
10-year periods beginning in 2028.
    S. 1532 contains no intergovernmental or
private-sector
mandates as defined in the Unfunded Mandates
Reform Act (UMRA).
As a condition of assistance, the bill would
require states to
ensure that individuals who commit acts of
human trafficking
are not issued commercial driver's licenses.
States already
screen applicants for a number of items,
including drug
offenses. Consequently, CBO estimates that the
costs of the
additional requirement would be small.
Conditions of
assistance, by definition in UMRA, are not
considered
intergovernmental mandates.
    The CBO staff contacts for this estimate
are Sarah Puro
(for federal costs) and Jon Sperl (for
intergovernmental
mandates). The estimate was approved by
Theresa Gullo,
Assistant Director for Budget Analysis.

Regulatory Impact

    In accordance with paragraph 11(b) of rule
XXVI of the
Standing Rules of the Senate, the Committee
provides the
following evaluation of the regulatory impact
of the
legislation, as reported:

number of persons covered

The bill affects commercial driver's license
(CDL) holders already subject to disqualifying
offenses at the Department of

Transportation. Therefore, the number of
persons covered would
be consistent with current levels. Further,
the disqualification that would be provided
under S. 1532 would potentially impact CDL
holders only if they were convicted of a
felony involving a severe form of trafficking
in persons.

economic impact

The legislation is not expected to have a
negative impact on the Nation's economy.

privacy

The reported bill is not expected to
impact the personal privacy of individuals.

paperwork

This legislation is not expected to result
in additional paperwork. S. 1532 would not
create any new programs, rather it
would provide an additional offense to
existing violations that warrant
disqualification for life under section 31310
of title 49, United States Code.

Congressionally Directed Spending

In compliance with paragraph 4(b) of rule
XLIV of the Standing Rules of the Senate, the
Committee provides that no provisions
contained in the bill, as reported, meet the
definition of congressionally directed
spending items under the rule.

Section-by-Section Analysis

Section 1. Short title.

This section would provide that the Act
may be cited as the

``No Human Trafficking on Our Roads Act.''

Section 2. Lifetime disqualification without reinstatement.

This section would amend section 31310(d) of title 49, United States Code, to include a lifetime disqualification without reinstatement for any individual who uses a CMV to commit a felony involving a severe form of trafficking in persons, as defined in paragraph (9) of 22 U.S.C. 7102.

Changes in Existing Law

In compliance with paragraph 12 of rule XXVI of the Standing Rules of the Senate, changes in existing law made by the bill, as reported, are shown as follows (existing law proposed to be omitted is enclosed in black brackets, new material is printed in italic, existing law in which no change is proposed is shown in roman):

TITLE 49. TRANSPORTATION

SUBTITLE VI. MOTOR VEHICLE AND DRIVER PROGRAMS

PART B. COMMERCIAL

CHAPTER 313. COMMERCIAL MOTOR VEHICLE OPERATORS

Sec. 31310. Disqualifications

(a) Blood Alcohol Concentration Level.--In this section, the blood alcohol concentration level at or above which an individual when operating a commercial motor vehicle is deemed to be driving under the influence of alcohol is .04 percent.

(b) First Violation or Committing Felony.--

(1) Except as provided in paragraph (2) of this
subsection and subsection (c) of this section, the Secretary of Transportation shall disqualify from operating a commercial motor vehicle for at least one year an individual-

(A) committing a first violation of driving a commercial motor vehicle under the influence of alcohol or a controlled substance;

(B) committing a first violation of leaving the scene of an accident involving a commercial motor vehicle operated by the individual;

(C) using a commercial motor vehicle in committing a felony (except a felony described in subsection (d) of this section);

(D) committing a first violation of driving a commercial motor vehicle when the individual's commercial driver's license is revoked, suspended, or canceled based on the individual's operation of a commercial motor vehicle or when the individual is disqualified from operating a commercial motor vehicle based on the individual's operation of a commercial motor vehicle; or

(E) convicted of causing a fatality through negligent or criminal operation of a commercial motor vehicle.

(2) If the vehicle involved in a violation referred to in paragraph (1) of this subsection is transporting hazardous material required to be placarded under section 5103 of this title, the Secretary shall disqualify the individual for at least 3 years.

(c) Second and Multiple Violations. --
(1) Subject to paragraph (2) of this subsection, the Secretary shall disqualify

from operating a commercial motor vehicle for
life an individual--
(A) committing more than one violation of
driving a commercial motor vehicle under the
influence of alcohol or a controlled
substance;

(B) committing more than one violation of
leaving the scene of an accident involving a
commercial motor vehicle operated by the
individual;

(C) using a commercial motor vehicle in
committing more than one felony arising out of
different criminal episodes;

(D) committing more than one violation of
driving a commercial motor vehicle when the
individual's commercial driver's license is
revoked, suspended, or canceled based on the
individual's operation of a commercial motor
vehicle or when the individual is disqualified
from operating a commercial motor vehicle
based on the individual's operation of a
commercial motor vehicle;

(E) convicted of more than one offense of
causing a fatality through negligent or
criminal operation of a commercial motor
vehicle; or

(F) committing any combination of single
 violations or use described in subparagraphs

(A) through (E).

   (2) The Secretary may prescribe regulations
establishing guidelines (including conditions)
under which a disqualification for life under
paragraph (1) of this subsection may be
reduced to a period of not less than 10 years.

(d) [Controlled Substance Violations] Lifetime

Disqualification Without Reinstatement. --[The
Secretary] (1) Controlled substance
violations.

--The Secretary shall disqualify from
operating a commercial motor vehicle for life
an individual who uses a commercial motor
vehicle in committing a felony involving
manufacturing, distributing, or dispensing a
controlled substance, or possession with
intent to manufacture, distribute, or dispense
a controlled substance.

(2) Human trafficking violations. -- The
Secretary shall disqualify from operating a
commercial motor vehicle for life an
individual who uses a commercial motor vehicle
in committing a felony involving an act
or practice described in paragraph (9) of
section 103 of the Trafficking Victims
Protection Act of 2000

(22 U.S.C. 7102(9)).
  (e) * * *

                              [all]

16

What if all the Irish left?

When you think of Irish, the first things that come to mind are JFK, Boston, lucky, St. Patrick's Day, beer, brawlers and red heads. The descendants of Ireland like many immigrants here in America have contributed tremendously to our society. One of the most noted Irish; Marry G. Harris Jones aka Mother Jones was educated as a schoolteacher but is known largely for being a labor, community organizer and activist.

President John F. Kennedy, Harvard graduate and politician resonated with American citizens as a potential great leader and was well on his way until his assassination on November 22, 1963 in Dallas, Texas. Former Vice president Joe Biden served with President Obama from 2009 to 2017.

Professional road racing cyclist Lance Armstrong won the World Championship in 1993 and went on to win several other championships including the Tour DuPont in 1995, 1996 and the Tour de France in 1999.

Unfortunately, allegations arise that Armstrong was doping which enabled him to win so many races. It wasn't until 2012 that the USADA aka United States Anti-Doping Agency concluded that the cyclist used performance enhancing drugs through-out his career.

When NFL quarterback; Tom Brady took over the starting position for the New England Patriot's it was a match made in heaven for the Irish. To date the QB has won 6 NFL Superbowl championships and continues to be active as the team's starter. In the early 1900's; Irish boxer, Jack Dempsey stunned crowds with his pugilist abilities while reigning as the world heavyweight champ from 1919 to 1926. Dempsey changed the sport of boxing once he garnered the first $1 million-dollar gate while boxing in front of sold out arenas.

Former NFL, Denver Bronco's quarterback; John Elway reigned as one of the best in the game during his career. Elway went on to win 2 Superbowl championships and currently sits as the General Manager for the Denver Broncos. Kevin McHale put the Irish in the Boston Celtics during his NBA career with his tough, smart and witty play. He went on to win 3 NBA

Championships during his career as a player. McHale also went on to coach the Minnesota Timberwolves and the Houston Rockets until 2015. He currently sits as an on-air analyst with NBA TV and Turner Sports. Professional Boxing owes a lot to former boxer and trainer; Freddie Roach. Roach has trained many great boxers and his work speaks for itself. Those boxers include; Manny Pacquiao, Oscar De La Hoya, Virgil Hill & Gary Stretch to name a few. He currently owns the World Card Boxing Club in Los Angeles.

The Irish cuisine can be found in most American households. Traditional dishes like corned beef and cabbage or lamb with roasted potatoes are considered hearty meals. Most meats are pork, like ham and bacon. Restaurants & Irish pubs can be found in all major cities where there's a strong Irish influence like Boston, New York and Los Angeles. Irish brown bread, skillet-roasted lamb loins with herbs, lemony salt-roasted fingerling potatoes, Irish buttered carrots, lamb and sweet potato shepherd's pie, Irish lamb and turnip stew, lobster and fennel salad are some of the top ordered dishes when dining at Irish pubs.

Industry titan; Henry Ford the founder of Ford Motor Company employed millions of Americans while introducing a line of cars that changed the way we traveled in our everyday lives. Ford made the automobile affordable to middle class America and found a way to meet supply and demand by implementing the assembly line technique to mass produce his cars. Paul Galvin co-founder of telecommunications company, Motorola also invented the car radio. The company was originally founded as Galvin Manufacturing Corporation in 1928.

The next time you eat a slice of domino's pizza, thank founder Tom Monaghan. He found the company in 1960 and it has become a household name, Tom also owned MLB's Detroit Tigers from 1983 -1992. Vince McMahon sits as the king of his own world. As the CEO of WWE aka World Wrestling Entertainment; McMahon has launched the careers of several superstars; Dwayne "The Rock" Johnson, The Undertaker, Triple H and Shawn Michaels to name a few. Millions tune in every week across the globe to be entertained by what he's created.

The Irish are considered blue bloods when it comes to law enforcement. It is not uncommon to find one family with several members serving the shield across America. Their commitment ranges from the everyday beat cop to the Chief Justice of Supreme court. Francis O'Neil trailblazed the way for Irish Americans when he was elected Chief of Police for the city of Chicago in 1901. Roger John Traynor followed suit and became the 23rd Chief Justice of California from 1964 to 1970. Roger I. McDonough served as the judge of the 3rd Judicial District Court from 1928 – 1938 and on the Utah Supreme Court from 1938 to 1966.

On the other end of the spectrum, for every Roger there was a James "Whitey" Bulger. During the 70's and most of the 90's, Whitey sat as the Mob Boss of the Winter Hill Gang and ran his organization with an iron fist. On June 22, 2011 Bulger was finally arrested by the FBI and charged with 32 counts of racketeering, money laundering, extortion, weapons charges and 19 murders. When it comes to organized crime, American Irish rival the top mafia families. Infamous gangsters like, Henry Hill, George Hogan, Jimmy Flynn and the McLaughlin brothers made sure that the FBI agents stayed employed in their cities.

The Irish rank among the most violent criminals in America. To protect their way of life, jobs or businesses the Irish would result to physical violence against anyone that wasn't Irish making moves on what was theirs. Considered poor immigrants when they first landed on American soil the Irish made the choice to separate themselves from other immigrants such as blacks and Latino's by joining forces with Anglo-Protestant hegemons or the whites and took up arms against the blacks to further prove their alliance. This was very important to the Irish because they were poor and at the bottom of the social class with the blacks. Over time, the Irish were no longer looked at as poor Irish immigrants. Many criminals begun the transition into law enforcement to clean up their poor immigrant image.

Their biggest problem still existed and wouldn't go away by trading races. Alcohol has always been their biggest downfall. Drunk Irish with bad attitudes weren't good for anyone. This led to more violent crimes and domestic abuse within the community. No matter how hard they tried, a large percentage of Irish found themselves on welfare, unemployed and in dead end jobs. This coupled with alcohol more times than none led to jail time.

Irish Americans has successfully implanted themselves as white Americans. Every walk of life and profession are filled with the descendants from Ireland, but you wouldn't know it unless you did the research. Grace Kelly, Mel Gibson, George Clooney, Jimmy Fallon, Tom Cruise, Jack Nicholson, John Cusack and Alec Baldwin are just a few people that are of Irish descent.

Now considered to be a part of mainstream America the Irish also fall into the larger percentage of Americans with the most buying power. If the Irish decided to leave and return to their home country. We would suffer a great deal; law enforcement positions would become depleted; the political landscape would shift along with the loss of some great presidents. The delicious Irish pubs, domino's pizza and all the great cuisine would be gone along with all the green beer and green rivers on St. Patrick's Day.

Can you imagine a world without car radios and all the Motorola products? No WWE! On the upside there will be much less whiskey and alcoholics in America.

17

Birds eye view.

As American citizens we often judge president Trump or any president for that matter from an emotional perspective. It's based on the current narrative of the overpopulated media and how you think his decisions effect you and your community. You take what he's saying as just bullshit or lies. In your vocation, you have a specific job or task that you must perform or complete every day while at work. During that time, you are the professional, you are privy to the information needed to do the job and you know all that it intel's. All the data needed for you to succeed is right there in front of you. So, it's safe to say that an outsider who's not privy to your information will not be successful in your vocation.

Just like you, the president has his own job to do and within this job he's able to see things from a bird's eye view. You or I could not pull up a real time chart on how many illegal immigrants are incarcerated or being detained for breaking the law. We cannot pull up a real time chart to see how much income American citizens have lost due to our companies and jobs relocating to other countries. We cannot see in real time, the staggering amount of money and aid that America has shelled out to so called allies whom never returned the favor.

President Trump who was once on the other side of the political spectrum is very familiar with the way D.C. works when it comes to lobbying money and getting things done. When he speaks, it's not from a position of ignorance like some of you would like to think but from a position of experience and awareness. Most of the media create the narrative that his message holds no validity. Stop for a minute and ask yourself, why would our president lie to us? What can he gain from telling a lie? When he sums up a statement by saying that things are very bad. It's not because he doesn't know but because the information is confidential, and he's only allowed to say very little. Let that sink in.

The difference between him and prior presidents is that they would not even answer or mention certain things. Trump speaks on everything no matter how you may feel about it. He tells it like it is, most of us just don't know how to swallow that.

18

What if the Italians left?

There's no way around it. When most people think of Italians, they think of great cuisine and la cosa nostra (The Mafia). It seems that the infamous have overshadowed the hard work and dedication that Italian American citizens have implanted here in the U.S.A. A crime element can be found within every immigrant culture but none so bracing as the Italians and their organized crime syndicate; the American mafia.

Angelo Bartlett Giamatti a distinguished professor of literature became the 19th president of Yale University from 12/20/1978 to 6/10/1986. Giamatti upon leaving Yale University crossed over into Major League Baseball when he was chosen to be their 14th National league president from 6/10/1986 to 4/1/1989. On the 1st of September 1989 he became the Commissioner of Baseball.

John J. DeGioia the 45th president of Georgetown University assumed office on 7/1/2001. He's won several awards, to include, "Brave Thinker" by The Atlantic, Lifetime Achievement Award for Excellence in Academia by the "Sons of Italy", and the "Catholic in the Public Square Award" by Commonweal.

Italian American & conservative; Lino Anthony Graglia despite his political acumen became infamous for these words; "blacks and Mexican-Americans can't compete academically with whites."

In the world of sports, the Italians rate among the best. Legendary athletes Rocky Marciano professional boxer reigned as the heavyweight champ from 1952 to 1956. Joe DiMaggio professional baseball player is noted as one of the most famous New York Yankees. Vince Lombardi is one of the best coaches to ever coach in the NFL. He never had a losing season during his coaching career, the current NFL Superbowl trophy is in his namesake. Lombardi coached the Green Bay Packers from 2/2/1959 to 2/1/1968 winning 3 NFL championships and the 1st two Superbowl's.

Ettore Boiardi aka Chef Hector Boyardee created the popular pasta brand that many Americans grew up on. Caesar Cardini; restaurateur, hotel owner and chef created what we now know as the Caesar salad which he and his brother originally served at their restaurant called Caesar's. American's have grown accustomed to several Italian American dishes like spaghetti, baked ziti, pizza, calzones, fettuccini, delicious salads and dressings, lasagna, veal, coffee, wine, cheeses, pane and pastries.

Did you know that the "Jacuzzi" was an American Italian family that created the whirlpool bath that we now know as the "Jacuzzi"? Seven brothers started the company Jacuzzi corporation in 1915 as a manufacture of wooden airplane propellers for the U.S. government and eventually evolved into a whirlpool and bubble bath manufacturer. Dr. Andrew Viterbi co-founder of Qualcomm, electrical engineer and inventor of the Viterbi algorithm has changed the way we communicate throughout the universe and even in space.

One doesn't need to look far to see the strange infatuation that American's have for organized crime. Film and screen adaptations like, The Godfather, Donnie Brasco, Casino, The Sopranos, Goodfellas and Boardwalk Empire pull in billions of dollars by exploiting American Italians and the organized crime mafia. For every athlete, actor, business owner, educator or inventor there must be at least 3; Lucky Luciano's, Al Capone's, Albert Anastasia's, Joe Columbo's or John Gotti's.

Individuals within our law enforcement and government has also benefited from the American mafia business. Taking down a criminal organization or the boss of a crime family warrants high accolades and job promotions. Prosecutor Thomas E. Dewey took down mobster Lucky Luciano, Eliot Ness and his Untouchables were sent out on a mission to capture Al Capone and any other mobsters they could tie up but it would be one of their own; Salvatore "Sammy the Bull" Gravano that took out John Gotti.

Like many other criminal organizations, the American Italians; specialized in extortion, murder, drug smuggling, prostitution, illegal gambling and any other scam that they could get their hands on.

In efforts to detain American Mafia mob bosses the government came up with the RICO law aka Racketeer Influenced and Corrupt Organizations Act. It was created for individuals who engaged with organized crime. A large percentage of American Italians are incarcerated today because of RICO. Because of its success, law enforcement found themselves using it on all organized crime organizations to include the blacks, Chinese, Japanese, Latino's and any crime organization involved in illegal gang activity.

If we could reverse all contributions made by the Italians. Organized crime as we know it, most likely wouldn't exist, murder rates would decrease tremendously, there would be far fewer corporate scams, etc. The delicious cuisine will probably be the thing that we miss most along with all the award-winning mafia film and movies. Let's face it, Americans love their guilty pleasures, no matter the cost.

19

Combating Human Trafficking in Commercial Vehicles Act.

On January 3, 2018; president Trump signed Act S.1536. The report reads as follows.

```
115th Congress
Report
                                      SENATE
1st Session
115-177
```

===
=========================

COMBATING HUMAN TRAFFICKING IN COMMERCIAL
VEHICLES ACT

R E P O R T

OF THE

COMMITTEE ON COMMERCE, SCIENCE, AND
TRANSPORTATION

ON

S. 1536

TRUMP this…

October 23, 2017.

--Ordered to be printed

U.S. GOVERNMENT PUBLISHING OFFICE
WASHINGTON: 2017

SENATE COMMITTEE ON COMMERCE, SCIENCE, AND TRANSPORTATION

One Hundred Fifteenth Congress
First Session

JOHN THUNE, South Dakota, Chairman
ROGER F. WICKER, Mississippi   BILL NELSON, Florida
ROY BLUNT, Missouri   MARIA CANTWELL, Washington
TED CRUZ, Texas   AMY KLOBUCHAR, Minnesota
DEB FISCHER, Nebraska   RICHARD BLUMENTHAL, Connecticut
JERRY MORAN, Kansas   BRIAN SCHATZ, Hawaii
DAN SULLIVAN, Alaska   EDWARD J. MARKEY, Massachusetts
DEAN HELLER, Nevada   CORY A. BOOKER, New Jersey
JAMES M. INHOFE, Oklahoma   TOM UDALL, New Mexico

MIKE LEE, Utah   GARY C.
PETERS, Michigan
RON JOHNSON, Wisconsin   TAMMY
BALDWIN, Wisconsin
SHELLEY MOORE CAPITO, West   TAMMY
DUCKWORTH, Illinois
    Virginia
CORY GARDNER, Colorado
MARGARETWOODHASSAN, NewHampshire
TODD C. YOUNG, Indiana
CATHERINE CORTEZ MASTO, Nevada
                    Nick Rossi, Staff
Director
            Adrian Arnakis, Deputy Staff
Director
                Jason Van Beek, General
Counsel
            Kim Lipsky, Democratic Staff
Director
        Christopher Day, Democratic Deputy
Staff Director

COMBATING HUMAN TRAFFICKING IN COMMERCIAL
VEHICLES ACT

                October 23, 2017.
--Ordered to be printed

Mr. Thune, from the Committee on Commerce,
Science, and Transportation, submitted the
following

                    R E P O R T

            [To accompany S. 1536]

[Including cost estimate of the Congressional Budget Office]

The Committee on Commerce, Science, and Transportation, to which was referred the bill (S. 1536) to designate a human trafficking prevention coordinator and to expand the scope of activities authorized under the Federal Motor Carrier Safety Administration's outreach and education program to include human trafficking prevention activities, and for other purposes, having considered the same, reports favorably thereon with an amendment (in the nature of a substitute) and recommends that the bill (as amended) do pass.

Purpose of the Bill

The purposes of S. 1536, the Combating Human Trafficking in Commercial Vehicles Act, are to designate a human trafficking prevention coordinator and to expand the scope of activities authorized under the Federal Motor Carrier Safety Administration's (FMCSA) outreach and education program to include human trafficking recognition, prevention, and reporting activities.

Background and Needs

Human trafficking, particularly sex trafficking, is known to be present at commercially operated truck stops and State-operated rest areas throughout the United States. Given their remoteness and insulation from communities, these locations can be convenient places for sex traffickers to operate with minimal concerns of detection. The frequent movement of these victims' aids traffickers both in maintaining control and avoiding law enforcement. Other forms of human trafficking, such as labor trafficking, have a presence in these locations as well.

Nonprofit organizations like Truckers Against Trafficking (TAT) have made substantial progress in spreading awareness of areas where human trafficking and the trucking industry intersect. Their efforts have resulted in increased reporting of trafficking incidents by truckers who can act as ``eyes and ears'' on roads nationwide. S. 1536 would provide additional tools to educate truckers and enlist their cooperation in preventing these crimes, while providing greater coordination between modal administrations of the Department of Transportation (DOT) to centralize efforts in combating human trafficking.

Summary of Provisions

S. 1536 would designate a human trafficking prevention coordinator at the DOT, responsible for managing prevention efforts across the modal administrations within the DOT and with other departments and agencies in the Federal Government, particularly those tailored to the transportation sector. S.1536 also would expand the scope of activities authorized under the DOT's FMCSA outreach and education program to include human trafficking prevention activities and provide eligibility under the FMCSA Commercial Driver's License (CDL) grant program to support the recognition, prevention, and reporting of human trafficking.

Finally, S. 1536 would create an advisory committee on human trafficking within the DOT, responsible for issuing legislative and administrative recommendations to the DOT while serving in an advisory capacity to State and local government agencies on human trafficking prevention strategies in the transportation sector.

107

Legislative History

S. 1536 was introduced on July 12, 2017, by Senators Klobuchar, Thune, and Nelson. Additional cosponsors include Senators Cornyn, Rubio, Heller, and Blumenthal. The Committee, by voice vote, ordered S. 1536 reported favorably with an amendment (in the nature of a substitute) on August 3, 2017.

In addition, on July 12, 2017, the Committee held a hearing entitled, ``Force Multipliers: How Transportation and Supply Chain Stakeholders Are Combating Human Trafficking,'' which examined the various interactions between the transportation sector and human trafficking and served as an opportunity to explore some of the specific solutions and efforts utilized by organizations that work to mitigate the exploitation of individuals.

Estimated Costs

In accordance with paragraph 11(a) of rule XXVI of the Standing Rules of the Senate and section 403 of the Congressional Budget Act of 1974, the Committee provides the following cost estimate, prepared by the Congressional Budget Office:

S. 1536--Combating Human Trafficking in Commercial Vehicles Act

S. 1536 would require the Department of Transportation (DOT) to designate an official to coordinate agency activities designed to prevent and address human trafficking, to establish an advisory committee on human trafficking within DOT, and to authorize that certain grant funds administered by the Federal Motor Carrier Safety Administration

(FMCSA) be used for activities related to preventing human trafficking. Based on information from DOT, CBO estimates that implementing the provisions of the bill would require an additional one to two employees per year over the 2019-2022 period at a cost of about $1 million over the 2018-2022 period, assuming availability of appropriated funds.

Enacting S. 1536 would not affect direct spending or revenues; therefore, pay-as-you-go procedures do not apply. CBO estimates that enacting S. 1536 would not increase net direct spending or on-budget deficits in any of the four consecutive 10-year periods beginning in 2028.

Under current law, FMCSA has $4 million per year in contract authority (a mandatory form of budget authority) to provide education and outreach grants. S. 1536 would make education about preventing and reporting of human trafficking an additional eligible expense for grant recipients. Because states already have flexibility to use their education and outreach grant funds, CBO does not expect the additional authority would have any significant effect on spending over the 2018-2022 period.

S. 1536 contains no intergovernmental or private-sector mandates as defined in the Unfunded Mandates Reform Act and would benefit state and local agencies by authorizing the use of federal assistance to support the prevention of human trafficking. Any costs incurred by those entities would result from voluntary commitments.

The CBO staff contact for this estimate is Sarah Puro. The estimate was approved by Theresa Gullo, Assistant Director for Budget Analysis.

Regulatory Impact Statement

TRUMP this...

In accordance with paragraph 11(b) of rule XXVI of the Standing Rules of the Senate, the Committee provides the following evaluation of the regulatory impact of the legislation, as reported:

NUMBER OF PERSONS COVERED

S. 1536 would not make any legislative modifications resulting in a change in the number of persons covered under existing law.

ECONOMIC IMPACT

The legislation is not expected to have a negative impact on the Nation's economy. Rather, the legislation would make changes within the DOT to increase awareness of human trafficking in the supply chain.

PRIVACY

The reported bill is not expected to impact the personal privacy of individuals.

PAPERWORK

This legislation is not expected to result in additional paperwork. While S. 1536 would create a DOT advisory committee on human trafficking, this and other modifications to existing law are not expected to result in more paperwork.

Congressionally Directed Spending

In compliance with paragraph 4(b) of rule XLIV of the Standing Rules of the Senate, the Committee provides that no provisions contained in the bill, as reported, meet the definition of congressionally directed spending items under the rule.

Section-by-Section Analysis

Section 1. Short title

This section would provide that the Act may be cited as the ``Combating Human Trafficking in Commercial Vehicles Act.''

Section 2. Human trafficking prevention coordinator

This section would establish a human trafficking prevention coordinator, responsible for coordinating human trafficking prevention activities throughout the modal administrations at the DOT and with other departments and agencies of the Federal Government.

Section 3. Expansion of outreach and education program

This section would authorize outreach and education funds for commercial motor vehicle safety also to be used for human trafficking recognition, prevention, and reporting purposes.

Section 4. Expansion of commercial driver's license financial assistance program

This section would provide eligibility under FMCSA's CDL grant program to support the recognition, prevention, and reporting of human trafficking.

Section 5. Establishment of the Department of Transportation Advisory

Committee on Human Trafficking

This section would establish the Advisory Committee on Human Trafficking (Advisory Committee) within the DOT. The Advisory Committee would consist of 15 external stakeholder members, with lifetime appointments, from trafficking advocacy organizations, law enforcement, and transportation modal sectors (e.g., trucking, maritime, and rail). The Advisory Committee would be charged with the submission of recommendations to the DOT on human trafficking, including prevention strategies and legislative or administrative changes.

Changes in Existing Law

In compliance with paragraph 12 of rule XXVI of the Standing Rules of the Senate, changes in existing law made by the bill, as reported, are shown as follows (existing law proposed to be omitted is enclosed in black brackets, new material is printed in italic, existing law in which no change is proposed is shown in roman):

TITLE 49. TRANSPORTATION

SUBTITLE VI. MOTOR VEHICLE AND DRIVER PROGRAMS

PART B. COMMERCIAL

CHAPTER 311. COMMERCIAL MOTOR VEHICLE SAFETY

SUBCHAPTER I. GENERAL AUTHORITY AND STATE GRANTS

Sec. 31110. Authorization of appropriations

(a) Administrative Expenses.

--There is authorized to be

appropriated from the Highway Trust Fund
(other than the Mass Transit Account) for the
Secretary of Transportation to pay
administrative expenses of the Federal Motor
Carrier Safety Administration—

        (1) $267,400,000 for fiscal year
2016;
        (2) $277,200,000 for fiscal year
2017;
        (3) $283,000,000 for fiscal year
2018;
        (4) $284,000,000 for fiscal year
2019; and
        (5) $288,000,000 for fiscal year
2020.
    (
b) Use of Funds. --The funds authorized by
this section shall be used for--
        (1) personnel costs;
        (2) administrative infrastructure;
        (3) rent;
        (4) information technology;
        (5) programs for research and
technology, information management, regulatory
development, and the administration of
performance and registration information
systems management under section 31106(b);
        (6) programs for outreach and
education under subsection (c);
        (7) other operating expenses;
        (8) conducting safety reviews of new
operators; and
        (9) such other expenses as may from
time to time become necessary to implement
statutory mandates of the Federal Motor
Carrier Safety Administration not funded
      from other sources.
    (c) Outreach and Education Program. --
        (1) In general. --The Secretary may
conduct, through any combination of grants,
contracts, cooperative agreements, and other
activities, an internal and external outreach
and education program to be administered by
the Administrator of the Federal Motor

Carrier Safety Administration. The program authorized under this subsection may support, in addition to funds otherwise available for such purposes, the recognition, prevention, and reporting of human trafficking, while deferring to existing resources, as practicable.

(2) Federal share. --The Federal share of an outreach and education project for which a grant, contract, or cooperative agreement is made under this subsection may be up to 100 percent of the cost of the project.

(3) Funding. --From amounts made available under subsection (a), the Secretary shall make available not more than $4,000,000 each fiscal year to carry out this subsection.

(d) Contract Authority; Initial Date of Availability. -- Amounts authorized from the Highway Trust Fund (other than the Mass Transit Account) by this section shall be available for obligation on the date of their apportionment or allocation or on October 1 of the fiscal year for which they are authorized, whichever occurs first.

(e) Funding Availability. --Amounts made available under this section shall remain available until expended.

(f) Contractual Obligation. --The approval of funds by the Secretary under this section is a contractual obligation of the Federal Government for payment of the Federal Government's share of costs.

CHAPTER 313. COMMERCIAL MOTOR VEHICLE OPERATORS

Sec. 31313. Commercial driver's license program implementation financial assistance program

(a) Financial Assistance Program. --
(1) In general. --The Secretary of Transportation shall administer a financial

assistance program for commercial driver's license program implementation for the purposes described in paragraphs (2) and (3).
(2) State commercial driver's license program implementation grants.--In carrying out the program,
the Secretary may make a grant to a State agency in a
fiscal year--
(A) to assist the State in complying with the requirements of section 31311; and
(B) in the case of a State that is making a good faith effort toward substantial compliance with the requirements of section 31311, to improve the State's implementation of its commercial driver's license program, including expenses--

(i) for computer hardware and software;
(ii) for publications, testing, personnel, training, and quality control;

(iii) for commercial driver's license program coordinators; and

(iv) to implement or maintain a system to notify an employer of an operator of a commercial motor vehicle of the suspension or revocation of the operator's commercial driver's license consistent with the standards developed under section 32303(b) of the

Commercial Motor Vehicle Safety Enhancement Act of 2012 (49 U.S.C. 31304 note).

(3) Priority activities. --The Secretary may make a grant to or enter into a cooperative agreement with a State agency, local government, or any person in a fiscal year for research, development and testing, demonstration projects, public education, and other special activities and projects relating

to commercial drivers licensing and motor
vehicle safety that--

(A) benefit all jurisdictions of the United
    States;

(B) address national safety concerns and
circumstances;

(C) address emerging issues relating to
 commercial driver's license improvements;

(D) support innovative ideas and solutions to
 commercial driver's license program issues;
                [or]

(E) support, in addition to funds otherwise
available for such purposes, the recognition,
prevention, and reporting of human
trafficking;
                or

[(E)](F) address other commercial driver's
license issues, as determined by the
Secretary.
   (b) Prohibitions. -- A recipient may not use
financial assistance funds awarded under this
section to rent, lease, or buy land or
buildings.

(c) Report. --The Secretary shall issue an
annual report on the activities carried out
under this section.

(d) Apportionment. --All amounts made
available to carry out this section for a
fiscal year shall be apportioned to a
recipient described in subsection (a)(3)
according to criteria prescribed by the
Secretary.

(e) Funding. --For fiscal years beginning
after September 30, 2016, this section shall
be funded under section 31104.

20

What if the Jews left?

A few things may come to mind when one thinks of Jewish Immigrants. Holocaust, Hollywood, Kosher foods, Finance, Shrewd but sharp business practices, Rabbi's & Bar mitzvahs. The Jews are among many immigrants that have strong religious and cultural beliefs. It's as if they govern themselves in an entirely different world within the United States.

Jewish American historian, Yosef Goldman co-authored one of the most important reference works in America; *Hebrew Printing in America 1735-1926: A History and Annotated Bibliography*. Howard Zinn; Historian, Playwright and Social thinker was chair of the history and social sciences department at Spelman College and a political science professor at Boston University.

Most noted Jewish American, Alan Greenspan served his country at the highest level when he served as chair of the Federal Reserve of the United States from 1987 to 2006. American lawyer and politician; William Roth will forever be remembered in history for his help in creating the Roth IRA, an individual retirement plan that can be set up by a broker.

The world of American sports has no shortage of Jewish athletes. Max Baer stunned many opponents during his reign as boxing's World Heavyweight Champion during 1934 -1935. Mark Spitz set several records as a competitive swimmer and won nine Olympic titles. His most noted achievement came during the 1972 Summer Olympics in Munich, West Germany when he won 7 Gold medals.

Sandy Koufax, Major League baseball player and Hall of famer, entertained millions of fans as the superstar lefthanded pitcher for the Brooklyn/Los Angeles Dodgers during 1955 - 1966. Bill Goldberg or shall I say Goldberg rose to the top of the wrestling world with WCW as the Heavyweight Champion from 1997-1998. Sue Bird, professional basketball player for the WNBA's Seattle Storm is considered one of the best players in the game. Her crown achievement this far comes in the form of three

WNBA championships; 2004, 2010 & 2018, four Olympic Gold medals; 2004, 2008, 2012 & 2016, four FIBA World Cups; 2002, 2010, 2014 & 2018 and two NCCA championships; 2000 & 2002 with UCONN.

Kosher food, cuisine that conforms to Jewish dietary laws forbids such foods as pork and shellfish, it also forbids one from eating meat and drinking milk at the same meal. So, if you go to a Jewish deli and ask for cheese on your sandwich, you're breaking the Jewish dietary laws, you sinner! Maybe a cheese sandwich with lettuce would be ok. This practice is totally optional it seems, because you can find a great number of Jewish American deli's that will serve you cheese with your meat. Afterall you do have that choice; "cheese or no cheese" when living in America.

Jews pride themselves on culture and religion. This must be conflicting for some business owners like the homosexual Harvey Levin; lawyer, tv producer and founder of paparazzi pushing, smut based tv and website; TMZ. Joseph Ainslie Bear the American banker held steady the Jewish financial trade as co-founder of investment bank Bear Stearns. Wall street is littered with hundreds of Jewish bankers and their hedge funds, the practice has become common place among the financial industry, in fact it is expected. Jewish Americans hold hundreds of executive positions at many of America's financial companies but is that a good thing? Can we trust Jews with American's money?

Jewish ran banks like Lehman Brothers, Goldman Sachs, Salomon Brothers, AIG and Citi Bank are just a few familiar names that controlled billions of America's cash and mortgages. Some closed their doors after the 2008 market crash largely due to bad mortgage loans and mishandling investor funds.

Several of America's professional sports franchises are owned by Jews. Mark Cuban, startup investor & Shark Tank host owns the Dallas Mavericks of the NBA. Joshua Harris, private equity investor owns the New Jersey Devils of the NHL and the Philadelphia 76ers of the NBA. Andrew Hauptman, founder of investor firm Andell Inc. owns the Chicago Fire Soccer Club of the MLS. Steven Kaplan, co-founder of Oaktree Capital Management is also a minority owner of the NBA's Memphis

Grizzlies. Barry Klarberg founder of Monarch Business & Wealth Management is the co-owner of MLB's New York Yankees. Seth Klarman, investor and hedge fund manager is a minority owner of MLB's Boston Red Sox. Joe Lacob, Silicon Valley Investor is co-owner of the NBA's Golden State Warriors. Marc Lasry, hedge fund manager and investor also co-owns the NBA's Milwaukee Bucks. Jonathan Lavine, investor and co-manager of Bain Capital is the co-owner of the NBA's Boston Celtics. Marc J. Leder, investor and co-founder of Sun Capital Partners, Inc. is also the co-owner of the NBA's Philadelphia 76ers. Al Lerner, former chairman of MBNA owns the NFL's Cleveland Browns.

Tony Ressler, co-founder of Apollo Global Management also owns the NBA's Atlanta Hawks. Rick Schnall, partner at Clayton, Dubilier & Rice is also a minority owner of the NBA's Atlanta Hawks. Bruce Sherman, wealth manager owns MLB's Miami Marlins. Futures and options trader Lee Sterns is also a minority owner of MLB's Chicago White Sox and former hedge fund manager; Jeffrey Vinik owns the Tampa Bay Lightning of the NHL. When it comes to the game of life in America, the Jews have certainly placed themselves in a winning position.

The same can be said for Jewish Americans in the underworld or on the illegal side of the equator shall I say. One Jew that's synonymous with organized crime or the American Mafia is the infamous Meyer Lansky. Lansky is known the world over as the mafia's accountant. During his reign in the Jewish Mob and as an associate of the American mafia he built a gambling empire with his involvement in the Las Vegas, London and Cuban casinos.

A few of America's key investment banks met their demise during the 2008 market crash, the ripple effect went on to wreck many lives but almost got overshadowed by the actions of investment advisor and financier; Bernie Madoff. During his time in the financial industry Bernie grew his firm to be worth over $64.8 million. He proved once again that Jews carry the highest acumen when it comes to finance but not the way everyone thought. Perhaps because of the governing body's complacency with the presumption that all Jewish financial firms are worthy, they turned a blind eye to Madoff's book of business and his practices until it was too late.

After being exposed by the market crash, Madoff decided to tell everyone that his firm has been running a Ponzi Scheme for the past 28 years. Thousands of investor funds were spent on the Madoff's luxury lifestyle for years and no one knew it. It's stated that his 48,000 investors lost an amount of $18 billion while Bernie Madoff were managing their funds. It is very important to note that the only reason Bernie got caught was because the impossible happened, the market crashed.

When most of his investors started calling to withdraw their funds, he knew the gig was up because he couldn't produce the money. Perhaps greed played a part in both sides of the spectrum; Bernie wanted to make more money and so did his investors. So, who can you blame? In America we have the right to make that choice but at our own peril.

It should come as no surprise that the American Stock Exchange was co-founded by a Jewish American; Carl Pforzheimer. During it's early inception in the 1960's the exchange experienced many cases of scandal or mismanagement and underwent reorganization in 1962 by hiring a new president and executive vice president to clean up the plagued American Stock Exchange. No matter how much history continues to repeat itself, some investors will never learn.

Several Jewish American financiers have been charged and convicted of insider trading, fraud, money laundering and Ponzi Schemes. In March 1989, the FED indicted financier Michael Milken on 98 counts of racketeering to include; misconduct, insider trading, stock parking and tax evasion. In January 1988, the FED indicted Barry Minkow on 54 counts of racketeering to include; money laundering, securities fraud, embezzlement, mail fraud, insider trading and tax evasion. In 1998, the FED indicted Jordan Belfort on securities fraud and money laundering. In 2002, the FED charged Andrew Fastow with 78 different counts of fraud, conspiracy and money laundering.

The fact of the matter is, the Jews have figured out the movement and attraction of money. They target the poor and wealthy alike by adding on fees for investments to higher interest rates for the poor, governing the management and mismanagement of money. I.e. if you overdraw your bank account and the bank charges you a $35 fee, that charge is a flat interest fee on a loan. (*You over charged $15 for gas on a 0-balance account and you will have to pay the bank a total of $50 to bring your balance current.*) The Jews are not the only race at the top of the financial industry, but they are the majority.

All American citizens have the right to government assistance if they qualify for it. While some fall below the poverty level and require assistance, there's always a few that find a way to cheat the system. According to charges and arrest made by the FBI, it's common practice for groups or organizations of Ultra-Orthodox Jews to understate their incomes to get free healthcare, food stamps, rental subsidies and other benefits. Records in one case showed a Jewish family of six reporting that they earned $39,000 a year so that they could collect government assistance. After further investigation the FBI found that the family earned over $1 million a year.

If all the Jews decided to leave America, white collar crime would be down, several professional sports teams would lose partners, a great deal of banks, investment firms and mortgage and loan companies would cease to exist. The entire kosher food market, jewelry, film and garment industry would suffer a great lost along with its consumers.

21

Twitter Fingers....

As humans we interact and converse with each other every day. Be it at work, home, the local grocery store or Church. When we speak, there's no buffers, the message gets delivered and received loud and clear. President's for the most part doesn't have that freedom when it comes to speaking to the American people, well that's the way it was before Trump. We all can identify with not believing the media and their narratives, they all want our attention so it could be turned into dollars.

We are blessed to live in a society where change is constant and encouraged. The purist way to connect with the American people for the president is his twitter account. There's no one writing a speech, script or trying to control the narrative. It's just him and us, and we can respond.

22

An Act to amend the Homeland Security Act of 2002 to require the Secretary of Homeland Security to issue Department of Homeland Security-wide guidance and develop training programs as part of the Department of Homeland Security Blue Campaign, and for other purposes.

On December 22, 2017; president Trump signed Act H.R.1370. The report reads as follows.

115th Congress
{Rept. 115-143}

HOUSE OF REPRESENTATIVES
 {1st Session }
Part 1

==
========================

DEPARTMENT OF HOMELAND SECURITY BLUE CAMPAIGN
AUTHORIZATION ACT OF 2017

_____

May 22, 2017. --Committed to the Committee
of the Whole House on the State of the Union
and ordered to be printed

———

Mr. McCaul, from the Committee on Homeland
Security, submitted the following

R E P O R T

[To accompany H.R. 1370]

The Committee on Homeland Security, to
whom was referred the bill (H.R. 1370) to
amend the Homeland Security Act of 2002
to require the Secretary of Homeland Security
to issue Department of Homeland Security-wide
guidance and develop training programs as part
of the Department of Homeland Security Blue
Campaign, and for other purposes, having
considered the same, report favorably thereon
with an amendment and recommend that the bill
as amended do pass.

CONTENTS

129

The amendment is as follows:
   Strike all after the enacting clause and insert the following:

SECTION 1. SHORT TITLE.

   This Act may be cited as the ``Department of Homeland Security Blue

Campaign Authorization Act of 2017''.

SEC. 2. ENHANCED DEPARTMENT OF HOMELAND SECURITY COORDINATION THROUGH

THE BLUE CAMPAIGN.

(a) In General. --Subtitle C of title IV of the Homeland Security Act of 2002 (6 U.S.C. 231 et seq.) is amended by adding at the end the following new section:

``SEC. 434. DEPARTMENT OF HOMELAND SECURITY BLUE CAMPAIGN.

``(a) In General. --There is authorized in the Department a campaign to be known as the `Blue Campaign'. As part of the Blue Campaign, the Secretary shall--

``(1) issue Department-wide guidance to appropriate personnel of the Department;

``(2) develop training programs for such personnel; and

``(3) coordinate departmental efforts, including training for such personnel.
``(b) Guidance and Training. --The Blue Campaign shall provide guidance and training to appropriate personnel of the Department regarding the following:

``(1) Programs for such personnel, as well as Federal, State, and local law enforcement entities, to help identify instances of human trafficking and potential connections to terrorist activities, including along the borders of the United States.

``(2) Systematic and routine information sharing between and among the components of the Department and the National Network of Fusion Centers regarding individuals suspected or convicted of human trafficking and patterns and practices of human trafficking and potential connections to terrorist activities, including along the borders of the United States.

``(3) Techniques to identify suspected victims of trafficking along the borders of the United States.

``(4) Techniques specifically for Transportation Security Administration personnel to--

``(A) identify suspected victims of trafficking at airport security; and

``(B) serve as a liaison and resource to aviation workers and the traveling public.

``(5) Utilizing resources to educate partners and stakeholders and increase public awareness of human trafficking, such as indicator cards, fact sheets, pamphlets, posters, brochures, and radio and television campaigns.

``(6) Leveraging partnerships with governmental, non-governmental, and private sector organizations at the State and local levels to raise public awareness of human trafficking and potential connections to terrorist activities, including along the borders of the United States.

``(7) Any other activities determined necessary by the Secretary as part of the Blue Campaign.
``(c) Definition. --In this section, the term `human trafficking' means an act or practice described in paragraph (9) or (10) of section 103 of the Trafficking Victims Protection Act of 2000 (22 U.S.C. 7102).''.
(b) Information Technology Systems. --Not later than one year after the date of the enactment of this Act, the Secretary of Homeland Security shall ensure that, consistent with the Department of Homeland Security-wide guidance required under subsection (a) of section 434 of the Homeland Security Act of 2002 (as added by subsection

(a) of this section), information technology
systems utilized within the Department
to record and track information regarding
individuals suspected or convicted of human
trafficking (as such term is defined in such
section 434) are integrated with each other.
    (c) Oversight. --Not later than 18 months
after the date of the
enactment of this Act, the Secretary of
Homeland Security shall report to the
Committee on Homeland Security of the House of
Representatives and the Committee on Homeland
Security and Governmental Affairs of the
Senate on the status and effectiveness of the
Blue Campaign.

    (d) Authorization. --There is authorized to
be appropriated $819,000 to carry out section
434 of the Homeland Security Act of 2002, as
added by subsection (a) of this section.
    (e) Clerical Amendment. --The table of
contents of the Homeland Security Act of 2002
is amended by inserting after the item
relating to section 433 the following new
item:

``Sec. 434. Department of Homeland Security
Blue Campaign.''.

                    Purpose and Summary

    This bill amends the Homeland Security Act
of 2002 (Pub. L. 107-296) to require the
Secretary of Homeland Security to issue
Department of Homeland Security-wide guidance
and develop training programs as part of the
Department of Homeland Security Blue Campaign
to combat human trafficking.

            Background and Need for Legislation

    Human trafficking is a multi-billion-
dollar industry that enslaves 20 million
people around the world whether for the

purposes of prostitution, sex exploitation, or forced labor. According to the FBI, the most effective way to investigate
human trafficking is through a collaborative, multi-agency approach with our Federal, State, local and tribal partners.DHS describe the Blue Campaign as a unified effort by the Department to conduct outreach to enhance awareness of
trafficking and provide training and materials to those in the best position to identify trafficking victims. The Campaign
works in collaboration with law enforcement, government, non-governmental and private organizations to identify victims and
trains others in identification techniques. The Department uses the resources and expertise of the Customs and Border Patrol, Immigration and Customs Enforcement, the U.S. Citizenship and Immigration Services, and the Federal Law Enforcement Training
Center to help with this effort.

This bill adds the Transportation Security Administration to this fight by training its personnel to recognize the signs of
trafficking and serve as a liaison to aviation workers and requires the Department to share information across the Department and with the National Network of Fusion Centers
regarding patterns and practices of human trafficking and potential connections to terrorist activities.

Hearings

No hearings were held on H.R. 1370 in the 115th Congress.

Committee Consideration

The Committee met on March 8, 2017, to consider H.R. 1370, and ordered the measure to be reported to the House with a
favorable recommendation, as amended, by voice vote. The Committee took the following

actions: The following amendments were
offered:

An amendment by Mr. Thompson of Mississippi
(#1) was AGREED TO by voice vote.
    Page 2, line 9, insert before ``As part
of the Blue Campaign'' the following: ``There
is authorized in the Department a campaign to
be known as the `Blue Campaign'.''.

Page 2, line 12, strike ``and'' after the
semicolon.

Page 2, line 14, strike the period and insert
``; and''.

Page 2, line 15, insert the following:

``(3) coordinate departmental efforts,
including training for such
personnel.''.

Page 2, beginning line 18, amend paragraphs
(1) and (2) to read as
follows:

``(1) Programs for such personnel, as well as
Federal, State, and local law enforcement
entities, to help identify instances of human
trafficking and potential connections to
terrorist activities, including along the
borders of the United States.

``(2) Systematic and routine information
sharing between and among the components of
the Department and the National Network of
Fusion Centers regarding individuals suspected
or convicted of human trafficking and patterns
and practices of human trafficking and

potential connections to terrorist activities, including along the borders of the United States.' '''.

Page 3, line 2, strike ``border'' and insert ``borders''.

Page 3, line 14, redesignate paragraph (6) as paragraph (7).

Page 3, beginning line 14, insert the following:

``(6) Leveraging partnerships with governmental, non-governmental, and private sector organizations at the State and local levels to raise public awareness of human trafficking and potential connections to terrorist activities, including along the borders of the United States.''.

Committee Votes

Clause 3(b) of Rule XIII of the Rules of the House of Representatives requires the Committee to list the recorded votes on the motion to report legislation and amendments thereto.

No recorded votes were requested during consideration of H.R. 1370.

Committee Oversight Findings

Pursuant to clause 3(c)(1) of Rule XIII of the Rules of the House of Representatives, the Committee has held oversight hearings and made findings that are reflected in this report.

New Budget Authority, Entitlement Authority, and Tax Expenditures

In compliance with clause 3(c)(2) of Rule XIII of the Rules of the House of Representatives, the Committee finds that H.R. 1370, the Department of Homeland Security Blue Campaign Authorization Act of 2017, would result in no new or increased budget authority, entitlement authority, or tax expenditures or revenues.

Congressional Budget Office Estimate

Pursuant to clause 3(c)(3) of Rule XIII of the Rules of the House of Representatives, a cost estimate provided by the Congressional Budget Office pursuant to section 402 of the Congressional Budget Act of 1974 was not made available to the Committee in time for the filing of this report. The Chairman of the Committee shall cause such estimate to be printed in the Congressional Record upon its receipt by the Committee.

Statement of General Performance Goals and Objectives

Pursuant to clause 3(c)(4) of Rule XIII of the Rules of the House of Representatives, H.R. 1370 contains the following general performance goals and objectives, including outcome related goals and objectives authorized.

The goal of H.R. 1370 is to authorize the DHS Blue Campaign to combat human trafficking.

Duplicative Federal Programs

Pursuant to clause 3(c) of Rule XIII, the Committee finds that H.R. 1370 does not contain any provision that establishes or reauthorizes a program known to be duplicative of another Federal program.

137

Congressional Earmarks, Limited Tax Benefits, and Limited Tariff

Benefits

In compliance with Rule XXI of the Rules of the House of Representatives, this bill, as reported, contains no congressional earmarks, limited tax benefits, or limited tariff benefits as defined in clause 9(e), 9(f), or 9(g) of the Rule XXI.

Federal Mandates Statement

An estimate of Federal mandates prepared by the Director of the Congressional Budget Office pursuant to section 423 of the Unfunded Mandates Reform Act was not made available to the Committee in time for the filing of this report. The Chairman of the Committee shall cause such estimate to be printed in the Congressional Record upon its receipt by the Committee.

Preemption Clarification

In compliance with section 423 of the Congressional Budget Act of 1974, requiring the report of any Committee on a bill or joint resolution to include a statement on the extent to which the bill or joint resolution is intended to preempt State, local, or Tribal law, the Committee finds that H.R. 1370 does not preempt any State, local, or Tribal law.

Disclosure of Directed Rule Makings

The Committee estimates that H.R. 1370 would require no directed rule makings.

Advisory Committee Statement

No advisory committees within the meaning of section 5(b) of the Federal Advisory

Committee Act were created by this
legislation.

Applicability to Legislative Branch

The Committee finds that the legislation
does not relate to the terms and conditions of
employment or access to public services or
accommodations within the meaning of section
102(b)(3) of the Congressional Accountability
Act.

Section-by-Section Analysis of the Legislation

Section 1.   Short Title.

This section provides that this bill may
be cited as the ``Department of Homeland
Security Blue Campaign Authorization
Act of 2017''.

Sec. 2.   Enhanced Department of Homeland
Security Coordination Through the Blue
Campaign.

This section amends the Homeland Security
Act by adding a new section authorizing the
Department's ``Blue Campaign'',
which shall issue guidance, develop training
to Department of Homeland Security (DHS)
personnel and coordinate Department-
wide training relating to the of human
trafficking. Through the DHS Blue Campaign,
the Secretary is authorized to provide
guidance and training on programs to help
identify instances of trafficking; systematic
and routine information sharing among
the components of the Department and the
National Network of Fusion Centers; techniques
to identify victims of trafficking
along the U.S. border; techniques for
Transportation Security Administration
personnel to identify victims of trafficking
and serve as a liaison and resource for

aviation workers and travelers; utilizing resources to promote public awareness of trafficking; and leveraging partnerships to raise public awareness of trafficking. The Secretary is also authorized to engage in additional activities necessary to operate the Blue Campaign. This section also includes a definition of human trafficking.

Additionally, this section directs the Secretary to ensure that, not later than 1 year after enactment, the information technology systems used for human trafficking-related information are integrated with each other. The Secretary shall also report to the House Committee on Homeland Security and the Senate Committee on Homeland Security and Governmental Affairs on the status and effectiveness of the Blue Campaign.

Last, the bill authorizes $819,000 to carry out the section and amends the table of contents of the Homeland Security Act with a clerical amendment.

Changes in Existing Law Made by the Bill, as Reported

In compliance with clause 3(e) of rule XIII of the Rules of the House of Representatives, changes in existing law made by the bill, as reported, are shown as follows (new matter is printed in italic and existing law in which no change is proposed is shown in roman):

HOMELAND SECURITY ACT OF 2002

SECTION 1. SHORT TITLE; TABLE OF CONTENTS.

(a) Short Title. --This Act may be cited as the ``Homeland Security Act of 2002''.
(b) Table of Contents. --The table of contents for this Act is

TRUMP this...

as follows:

* * * * * * *

TITLE IV--BORDER, MARITIME, AND TRANSPORTATION
SECURITY

* * * * * * *

Subtitle C--Miscellaneous Provisions

* * * * * * *

Sec. 434. Department of Homeland Security Blue
Campaign.

* * * * * *

TITLE IV--BORDER, MARITIME, AND TRANSPORTATION
SECURITY

* * * * * *

Subtitle C--Miscellaneous Provisions

* * * * * *

SEC. 434. DEPARTMENT OF HOMELAND SECURITY BLUE
CAMPAIGN.

(a) In General. --There is authorized in the
Department a campaign to be known as the
``Blue Campaign''. As part of the
Blue Campaign, the Secretary shall--
(1) issue Department-wide guidance
to appropriate personnel of the Department;
(2) develop training programs for
such personnel; and
(3) coordinate departmental efforts,
including training for such personnel.
(b) Guidance and Training. --The Blue
Campaign shall provide guidance and training
to appropriate personnel of the

Department regarding the following:

(1) Programs for such personnel, as well as Federal, State, and local law enforcement entities, to help identify instances of human trafficking and potential connections to terrorist activities, including along the borders of the United States.

(2) Systematic and routine information sharing between and among the components of the Department and the National Network of Fusion Centers regarding individuals suspected or convicted of human trafficking and patterns and practices of human trafficking and potential connections to terrorist activities, including along the borders of the United States.

(3) Techniques to identify suspected victims of trafficking along the borders of the United States.

(4) Techniques specifically for Transportation Security Administration personnel to--

(A) identify suspected victims of trafficking at airport security; and

(B) serve as a liaison and resource to aviation workers and the traveling public.

(5) Utilizing resources to educate partners and stakeholders and increase public awareness of human trafficking, such as indicator cards, fact sheets, pamphlets, posters, brochures, and radio and television campaigns.

(6) Leveraging partnerships with governmental, non-governmental, and private sector organizations at the State and local levels to raise public awareness of human trafficking and potential connections to terrorist activities, including along the borders of the United States.

(7) Any other activities determined necessary by the Secretary as part of the Blue Campaign.
  (c) Definition. --In this section, the term ``human trafficking'' means an act or practice described in paragraph

(9) or (10) of section 103 of the Trafficking Victims Protection Act of 2000 (22 U.S.C. 7102).

23
What if all the Latino & Hispanic's left?

Latin Americans make up a large percentage of our minority population. The descendants of Mexico, Puerto Rico, Dominican Republic, Cuba, etc. Today it's not strange to see two language signs posted in your local businesses; English & Spanish. If you find yourself in the position of having the ability to read and speak them both, well you certainly have the advantage. Don't you?

If America was at war with the Latino's then they would be winning by a large margin. The lifestyle and culture of Latin America has entrenched itself deep into our way of life. Spanish is the second largest language spoken in the United States behind the English language. When you make a business phone call you get greeted in English and Spanish. No other minority has entrenched themselves into the American culture to that extent. Most jobs will pay a bilingual candidate more than one whom only speaks one language and the preferred second language is always, Spanish.

It is true that most minorities have their own sections of neighborhoods through-out the U.S. where you can go to experience their culture, but the Hispanic's far surpass any of them on a national scale. When you turn on your television and or radio you will find two listening or viewing options. Yep, that's English or Spanish, they even have their own networks. For every ESPN, there's an ESPN deportes, for every HBO, there's an HBO Latino.

America is the land of opportunity and if you know how to play the game you can take advantage of those many opportunities. So, it's not so farfetched to foresee a United States where the Latin Americans are the dominate race. Add in, the increasing amounts of illegal Latino immigrants sneaking across our borders every minute and the picture will start to become clearer. We are indeed, under attack and the opposition is well organized despite your benighted or cultured opinion.

Hispanics have contributed to America's society in more ways than one whether good or bad. Martha E. Bernal led the way in education by becoming the first Mexican American to receive a psychology PHD in the United States. Melba J. T. Vasquez also followed suit by becoming the 1st Latina of the American Psychological Association. Miguel Algarin co-founder of the Nuyorican Poets Café in lower Manhattan, New York has contributed tremendously to the artistic world.

Angel Taveras made history as the first Hispanic mayor of Providence, Rhode Island. Latino's are growing at a steady pace within the world of politics, giving a much-needed voice to the Hispanic population. Grace Diaz, Adriano de Jesus Espaillat Cabral & Alexandria Ocasio-Cortez are just a few Hispanics elected as U.S. Representatives for their states. Billionaire, Marcelo Claure and founder of BrightStar the mobile device distributor serving more than 200 carriers in 50 countries trailblazed the entrepreneur path for many Hispanic Americans.

Tony Jimenez, founder of MicroTech, Maria Contreras-Sweet founding Chairwoman of ProAmerica commercial Latino bank of California, founder of Hotels.com, Expedia.com

& AutoWeb.com; Matias de Tezanos and Martha de la Torre, founder of El Clasificado are great examples of successful entrepreneurs and business owners.

Latin and Hispanic Americans are represented at the highest level in the world of sports when it comes to soccer and baseball. Superstar players like; David Ortiz, Sammy Sosa, Pedro Martinez, Robinson Cano and Albert Pujols are a few players that were recruited by Major League Baseball away from their home countries. When America wants something or someone from another country, we have a way to impose our will and more times than none, we do get our way. Soccer however is a different story, America had to create a platform to showcase the otherwise global sport that the growing population of Latin and Hispanic Americans enjoy.

It fell right into our way of doing things, a demand was being created for a product and it was time to deliver. Elementary, middle, high school and intermural soccer programs popped up all over the nation. It's no accident that America now has several amateur and professional soccer leagues in every city and state. The establishment of the fore mention rolled out the red carpet for soccer players & leagues across the globe. This brought on tremendous financial opportunities and we have the Latin and Hispanic Americans to thank for it. Isn't America a great place to live!

Some of the most delicious cuisine in America comes from the Latin and Hispanic culture. Churrasco, a Spanish term used to describe beef or grilled meat can be found through-out America in Brazilian steakhouses. Feijoada, a flavorful Brazilian stew consisting of black beans, pork or beef, served with rice, vegetables and a variety of sausage is a favorite in Latin American circles. Most common in the U.S. would be the *Tamal* or Tamale in American a fulfilling Latin snack made of a starchy corn-based dough filled with meats, cheeses, fruits, vegetables or chilies, then steamed or broiled in a leaf paper.

Another is the Empanada, a baked or fried bread or pastry stuffed with meat, cheese, corn smut, fruit or vegetables. Not to be forgotten are all the spices we use daily to prepare or spice up our meals. Cilantro, jalapeno's, cumin, saffron, cinnamon, cloves and paprika are among the most used here in America.

According to the U.S. Bureau of Justice Statistics, Hispanics make up 20.6% of incarcerated males in America. Leading the rate for most incarcerated are the blacks with Hispanics coming in at a close second with the whites. Most are incarcerated for violent crimes such as murder, assault, drug distribution and armed robbery.

The Hispanics however lead the way when it comes to crimes related to gang activity. Latino gangs make up 46% of the active gangs here in the United States, the blacks follow with 35%. We can safely assume that this number will continue to increase with the constant overflow of illegal Latino and Hispanic immigrants crossing our borders at alarming rates. This will of course inflate violent crimes like murder, armed robbery, assault and all related drug offenses. A statistic we don't need or want.

The most dangerous of them all, MS-13 has a global reach in the world of crime. Led by former law enforcement and or military personnel, the gang has strategized its mission to take advantage of several global territories not to exclude the United States.

Proficient in drug trafficking, human smuggling, prostitution, murder for hire, auto theft and many other crimes. MS-13 is and will continue to be a threat to our way of life and the U.S. economy. They are strengthening at a rapid pace while controlling the trafficking corridors to and from America among other places.

Latino's rate among the highest citizen's using public housing and are the second highest race living below the poverty level in America according to the 2017 census bureau. The average working Hispanic American earns about $50,000.00 year, $10,000.00 above working blacks who average $40,000.00 a year rating as the lowest earning American's in the country.

According to the FBI 2017 UCR, Hispanic's committed 27% of rape crimes, 26.1% of motor vehicle thefts, 24.5% of gambling offenses, 23.5% of violent crimes, 24.3% of sex offenses, 22.8% of weapon's possession, 22.5% of DUI's, 21% of burglaries and 20.7% of prostitution crimes.

If the Latin population decided to return to their home countries it would not go unnoticed. Baseball and soccer teams will decrease tremendously at all levels. Media networks along with every other line of business will see their bottom lines decline immediately, bilingual customer service departments will become English speaking only. Bilingual signs that are posted in restaurants, airports, bus stations and other public buildings would be no more.

Many violent crimes will disappear along with a large amount of law enforcement jobs. Man-hours at the U.S. borders would be cut largely because Latino's make up the most immigrants sneaking across our borders. The delicious Hispanic and Latin cuisine that has entrenched itself within American culture with all its spices would leave a bland taste on our palettes. Hell, we won't even have to worry about building the wall any longer. If only, it was that easy.

24

10 Reasons why we need the Wall.

1. When an illegal immigrant commits a crime in the United States, they have the luxury of returning home on our dime, no less. An American will be indicted, charged and convicted then labeled as a felon for eternity. An illegal immigrant will give themselves a new name then sneak back across the border into America and commit more crimes until they get caught or not get caught; it's as if they have carte blanche. These crimes include murder, rape, drug and human trafficking, burglary, etc.

2. Millions of hardworking American citizens lose their jobs every hour to illegal immigrants that are willing to work for lower wages.

3. In most Latin and Hispanic countries there no laws for having sex with minors. They bring those same morals with them when they illegally cross our borders, endangering little girls and boys every day.

4. Some auto insurance companies in the United States (Progressive, Infinity, Gainsco) will cover illegal immigrants with or with-out a driver's license as long as they have an international identification card or passport while any American citizen is required to have a license before they can get their registered vehicle insured.

5. American citizens are required to pay taxes on their income while illegal immigrants are being paid cash under the table and away from the eyes of the IRS.

6. In California, immigrants from 3rd world countries make up 51% of people on any kind of government assistance. The other 49% are tax paying voters. The democrats are pushing to give voting rights to the illegal aliens, clearly so that they could have an advantage over the republican party.

7. Prostitution is legal in the Latin and Hispanic countries. Their women have become one of their biggest commodities which has led to a dramatic increase in human trafficking of Latin and Hispanic

women into the United States to work in the billion-dollar sex industry. (*Also includes Asian women*)

8. Latin and Hispanic gangs and cartels have taken a strong hold of our borders and continue to sneak their soldiers (narcos, cartel & gang members) into our country to increase their power within the criminal underworld. They have organized themselves to fit into American society to control the illegal drug, sex and human trafficking trades.

9. Most illegal immigrants enter the United States through Mexico and are from Central America, Honduras & Guatemala. Not to be excluded are Asia, Africa, China, Ethiopia, Ghana, India & South Korea. However, the biggest influx of illegal immigrants is of Latin and Hispanic descent. (*There currently an estimate of 15 million illegal immigrants in the United States*)

10. The democrats are quick to pull the sympathy card when it comes to our borders, the wall and detaining immigrants but not one democrat took the president up on his invite when he

offered to bus the illegal immigrants out of the detention centers or camps and into their democratic Sanctuary Cities.

MAKE AMERICA GREAT AGAIN!